A CLOSE READING

ACKNOWLEDGEMENTS
Some of these versions first appeared in *Cardinal Points*, *The Manchester Review*, *PN Review*, *Poetry Review*, *The Wolf*, *The Assay*, *After Semyon Izrailevich Lipkin*, *Yvonne Green's Selected Poems and Translations*, *Jam & Jerusalem* and were included in the *Penguin Book of Russian Poems*. I thank all the editors and publishers concerned.

ALSO BY YVONNE GREEN
Testimony from the Literary Memoirs of Semyon Izrailevich Lipkin (Hendon Press, 2023)
Jam & Jerusalem (Smith|Doorstop, 2018)
Honoured (Smith|Doorstop, 2015)
Selected Poems and Translations (Smith|Doorstop, 2014)
After Semyon Izrailevich Lipkin (Smith|Doorstop, 2011)
The Assay (Smith|Doorstop, 2010)
Boukhara (Smith|Doorstop, 2008)

Anthologies:
The Penguin Book of Russian Poetry (Penguin, 2015)
Russia is Burning – Poems of the Great Patriotic War (Hachette, 2020)
Mapping Faith: Theologies of Migration and Community (Jessica Kingsley, 2020)
Resistance – Voices of Exiled Writers (Palewell Press, 2020)

A CLOSE READING

OF FIFTY-THREE POEMS BY
SEMYON IZRAILEVICH LIPKIN

Selected by
Alexander Solzhenitsyn

Translated by
Yvonne Green
and **Sergei Makarov**

With an introduction by
Professor Donald Rayfield

Published 2023 by
Hendon Press
21 Wykeham Road,
Hendon,
London
NW4 2TB

ISBN 978-1-739778-52-1

British Library Cataloguing-in-Publication Data.
A catalogue record for this book is available from the
British Library.

Designed & Typeset in the UK by Utter

Inner cover image: The blue-washed, clay-walled
houses of Krasnodar ©Prof. Brigid O'Keeffe
https://brigidokeeffe.com

CONTENTS

ENGLISH VERSIONS OF THE POEMS CITED BY
ALEXANDER SOLZHENITSYN

ב״ה

For Brian and all we build

CHRONOLOGY OF HISTORICAL EVENTS DURING LIPKIN'S LIFE

1911, September 6 (Julian Calendar)
Semyon Izrailevich Lipkin born 19 September 1911 (Gregorian Calendar), Odesa; son of Israel and Rosalia Lipkin; his father had a tailoring business.

1914, June 28
Franz Ferdinand, Archduke of Austria and his wife are assassinated in Sarajevo by Gavrilo Princip, the *casus belli* of the First World War.

1917   Bolshevik revolution.

1918–20   Civil war.

1921–22   Famine in Volga basin.

1924   Death of Lenin. Petrograd is renamed Leningrad. Stalin begins to take over power.

1925   Lipkin's first poem published, age 15. Eduard Bagritsky recognises the merit of this first publication.

1930, February
Central Committee Decree calls for the liquidation of the Kulaks as a class.

April 14   Mayakovsky commits suicide.

1931   Stalin orders enforced collectivization. Kalmyk Buddhist monasteries closed, and religious texts burned.

1932   Independent literary groups closed, and Union of Soviet Writers formed.

1932–34   Between eight and ten million peasants killed by their own government's Terror Famine (*Holodomor*) in Ukraine, Volga basin, Kalmyk

ASSR and elsewhere in the Soviet Union.
Shostakovich's *Lady Macbeth of Mtsensk*
denounced.

1936–38 Approximately half the members of the Soviet
political, military and intellectual elite are
imprisoned or shot. Around 380,000 supposed
'Kulaks' are killed, as are around 250,000 members
of various national minorities.

1937 Lipkin graduates from the Moscow Economics
Engineering Institute. While studying engineering
he had begun studying Farsi, followed by other
Oriental languages including Dagestani, Kalmyk,
Kyrgyz, Tatar, Tajik, Uzbek, Kabardian, Yiddish
and Moldavian; also their history and culture
including Islam and Buddhism.

1939–41 Death of 70,000 mentally handicapped Germans in
the Nazis' euthanasia programme.

1939 Nazi-Soviet pact. Beginning of Second World War.

1941 Germany invades the Soviet Union. Leningrad
is blockaded and Moscow under threat. Two and
half million Polish Jews are gassed in Chelmno,
Majdanek, Belzec, Sobibor, Treblinka and
Auschwitz. Lipkin's friend, Vasily Grossman, starts
work as a war correspondent for *Red Star* (*Krasnaya
Zvezda* – the Red Army newspaper).

1941–42 Two million Jews are shot in western areas of the
Soviet Union; Grossman's mother is one of the
approximately twelve thousand Jews killed in a
single day at the airport outside Berdichev.

1941–45 Lipkin served in the Red Army, including at
Stalingrad.

1941, September 8
Siege of Stalingrad begins.

1942–1943, August to February
Battle of Stalingrad.

1942, December
Soviets reconquer the Kalmyk ASSR.

1943, July/August
Decisive Soviet victory at the Battle of Kursk.

1943   Stalin declares all Kalmyks to be Nazi collaborators. In December the total population of the Kalmyk ASSR, including communists, is deported to prison camps in Siberia and Central Asia.

1944, January 27
Siege of Stalingrad lifted.

1944, April–June
436,000 Hungarian Jews are gassed at Auschwitz, in only fifty-six days.

1944, August–October
Warsaw uprising.

1945, January 27
Liberation of Auschwitz.

1945, May 9
Surrender of Germany.

1946   Nuremberg Trial of the Nazi leadership. In the Soviet Union, Andrey Zhdanov tightens control over the arts.

1948   Murder of Solomon Mikhoels, head of the Jewish Anti-Fascist Committee, which was then dissolved. The plates for the Soviet edition of *The Black Book*, a documentary of the Final Solution in the Soviet Union and Poland, compiled by Ilya Ehrenburg and Grossman between 1943–1946 were destroyed.

| 1953 | Publication of article in *Pravda* in January about the Jewish "Killer Doctors." Preparations continue for Stalin's purge of Soviet Jews. March 5: Death of Stalin. April 4: Official acknowledgement that the case against the 'Killer Doctors' is fabricated. |

1956, February

Nikita Khrushchev's Secret Speech to the Communist Party. He denounces the forcible exile of the Kalmyks, Karachai, Chechen, Ingush, and Balkhars.

1956, Oct–Nov

Suppression of Hungarian insurrection.

| 1957 | Some Kalmyks allowed to return. |

| 1958 | The former Kalmyk ASSR reconstituted. Boris Pasternak's *Dr Zhivago* is published abroad. Under pressure from the Soviet authorities he declines the Nobel Prize. |

1960, October

Against the advice of Yekaterina Vasilievna Zabolotskaya and Lipkin, Vasily Grossman submits his novel *Life and Fate* for publication to the editors of *Znamya*.

| 1961 | The KGB raid Grossman's home and destroy all the copies of *Life and Fate* they can. Lipkin keeps one copy at Peredelkino and later transfers it to Sergei and Lena Makarov's attic in Moscow for safe keeping. Unbeknown to Lipkin, Lyola Klestova has been given the original manuscript by Grossman who arranges prior to his death for her to give her copy to Vyacheslav Loboda. |

1962, November

Alexander Solzhenitsyn's *One Day in the Life of Ivan Denisovich* published in the Soviet Union.

1964   Fall of Khrushchev; death of Vasily Grossman.

1966   Trial of Andrei Sinyavski and Yuli Daniel.

1967   Lipkin receives the Rudaki State Prize of the Tadzhik SSR. Lipkin's first collection of poetry *Ochevidets* [*Eyewitness*] published. His poem 'Conjunction' is read as coded support for Israel.

1968, August
      Warsaw Pact invasion of Czechoslovakia.

1968   Lipkin made People's Poet of the Kalmyk ASSR.

1970   First issue of Jewish samizdat journal *Exodus*. Lipkin's *A Notebook of Being* published.

1971   Beginning of permitted Jewish emigration.

1973   Solzhenitsyn's *Gulag Archipelago* published in Paris.

1974   Solzhenitsyn exiled from the USSR.

1975   Andrei Sakharov awarded Nobel Peace Prize. Lipkin's *Vechnyi Den'* [*Eternal Day*] published. Lipkin asks the writer Vladamir Voinovich to help him get his copy of *Life and Fate* (the manuscript) published in the West. Voinovich inexpertly microfilms the manuscript but then gets Sakharov to make a better microfilm. The latter film reaches the Parisian dissident journal *Kontinent* via Russia's Austrian attaché. Only extracts are published.

1977   Voinovich microfilms the manuscript again and it reaches Yefim Etkind and Shimon Markish via the Austrian Professor Rosemary Zeigler.

1979   Lipkin and Inna Lisnyanskaya submit their poetry to the anthology, *Metropol*, which is rejected by the Soviet authorities.

1980   Lipkin resigns from the Union of Writers. Internal exile of Sakharov. Grossman's *Life and Fate* published in Switzerland, from Voinovich's films of the manuscript as painstakingly collated by Etkin and Markish.

1981   *Metropol* published in the United States. Lipkin's *Volya* [*Free Will*] published in Russian in the US on the initiative of Joseph Brodsky.

1982   Death of Leonid Brezhnev.

1984   Death of Yuri Andropov. Lipkin's *Kochevi Onon'* [*A Nomadic Flame*] published in Russian in US.

1985   Mikhail Gorbachev becomes general secretary of the Communist Party of the Soviet Union. The period known as Perestroika begins. Loboda's widow shows the original manuscript of *Life and Fate* to Fyodor Guber and it was used to correct textual lacunae in the Swiss version before *Life and Fate* was first published in Moscow. The first publication in Russia of *Life and Fate* along with Grossman's *Everything Flows* and important works by Sigizmund Krzhizhanovsky, Andrey Platonov, Varlam Shalamov, Solzhenitsyn and many others.

1986   Lipkin's *Kartiny i golosa* [*Pictures and Voices*] published in Russian in London. Lipkin is reinstated into the Writers' Union.

1988   Pasternak's *Doctor Zhivago* published in Soviet Union. October: Gorbachev becomes president.

1989, *November*
        Fall of Berlin Wall.

1991   Dissolution of USSR. Lipkin awarded Tukai Prize. His *Lunnyi Svet* [*Moonlight*] and *Pis'mena* [*Letters*] are published.

1992   Outbreak of civil war in Tajikistan.

1993   Boris Yeltsin suppresses armed rising by Supreme
             Soviet.

1995   Lipkin awarded the Sakharov Prize by the
             European Parliament, and the Pushkin Prize by the
             Alfred Toepfer Foundation, Germany.

1997   Lipkin's *Posokh* [*Shepherd's Crook*] published.

2000   Putin elected president. Lipkin's *Sem' desiatiletii*
             [*Seven Decades*] published.

2003, May 31
             Death of Semyon Izrailevich Lipkin at Peredelkino.

PREFACE

This book comprises a translation, with endnotes, of Alexander Solzhenitsyn's article on Lipkin's poems first published in *Novy Mir* (Moscow, No4, 1998). I am indebted to Natalia Solzhenitsyn for granting me permission to translate, to Inna Lisnyanskaya for obtaining that permission, to Professor Donald Rayfield for encouraging me to translate the forty poems Solzhenitsyn quotes, and to Lipkin's son-in-law, the writer and historian, Sergei Makarov for his literal versions and extensive insights and erudition.

In essence, Makarov and I are each reading Solzhenitsyn on Lipkin for English readers. Translation and critical appraisal merge here as acts of appreciation.

I read Lipkin's widow, Inna Lisnyanskaya's poetry in the translation, *Far From Sodom* (Daniel Weissbort, Arc Publications, 2005), and loved its perception, in particular the glimpses of her late husband's insight.

Only a handful of Lipkin's poems had been translated, so by audio taping Russian friends reading them and using literal translations obtained word by word, line by line, most notably from Sergei Makarov, and by examining the evident patchwork of rhyme visible on the page and with the help of a phonetic copy of the Cyrillic alphabet, I began my search to understand Lipkin's poems and bring them to an English reader.

The project has taken me twenty years, and I'm indebted to many people along the road. Lipkin's work was informed by three sources; his personal experience of war (he served at Stalingrad), his friend Vasily Grossman's reports of Treblinka, and his encyclopedic knowledge of the languages and history of Central Asia. He translated from Buriat, Dagestani, Farsi, Kalmyk, Kabardian, Kirghiz, Tatar, Tadjik, and Uzbek.

Lipkin preserved cultures that Sovietization undermined by translating their poetry into Russian, the Bibliography of his work I've appended shows these. These included versions of the Kalmyk epic *Dzhangar* (1940), the Kirghiz epic *Manas* (1941), the Kabardian epic *Narty* (1951), the Buriat epic *Geser* (1968), and the classic works of the classical Tadzhik, Uzbek, Kirghiz, Balkar, and Kalmyk poets. His translations were published as *Kabardian Epic Poetry* (1956), *Voices of Six Centuries* (1960), and *The Golden Chain: Eastern Poems* (1970). Lipkin received prizes detailed in the Chronology of this book as well as four orders and a number of medals.

He was not alone amongst his beleaguered compatriots, some of whom also translated when their poems were banned, but his work was recognized by Tsvetaeva and Brodsky to have been unique. They singled out his own poetry beyond his generous œuvre of translation, which until Perestroika was read in manu-script or heard recited from memory by very few.

Sergei Makarov told me, "Lipkin knew about everything, politics, economics, culture, religion." Inna said, slicing the air above her head with her slim, vermillion-manicured hand, "He loved people who loved God." Which I took to mean who understood they weren't supreme.

If my translations succeed in no other respect, I hope they show how Lipkin recognized supremacism and loathed it.

Thanks are due to Sharon Dewinter, Gila Pfeffer, and others who helped and encouraged me to fledge this book, and to Abigail Hayton for our discussions on the project. Inna Lisnyanskaya and her daughter Lena Makarova gave me generous and patient support from the outset. Lena works tirelessly documenting the thousands of lectures, plays, operas, concerts, and works of fine art produced at Tereizen by inmates who went on to their deaths. Every moment she gave me was beyond value. Finally, many thanks are due to my assistant, Keith Lauchlan, for his careful editing and preparation of this volume.

There are many theories about how translation should be approached; Nabokov's line-by-line with footnotes; Brodsky's insistence that rhyme and meter be reproduced faithfully; sense being secondary (*From Russian With Love*, Daniel Weissbort, Anvil Press Poetry, 2004); and recently echoed by John Ashberry (see a discussion of this in *The North* No.53, The Poetry Business); Hughes' assertion that translation should not be smooth; the current fashion for intuited translated. 'Moldavian is a Language' is an example of an attempt I have made to mimic form; on the whole, I've tried to convey the internal conversation of Lipkin's work. Any failures are my own and not those of my co-translator.

Lipkin's work has now been included in *The Penguin Book of Russian Poetry* (Edited by Robert Chandler, Boris Dralyuk, and Irina Mashinski, Penguin Classics, 2015). My hope is that other writers will make their own versions of Lipkin's supremely classical poems. His use of form and language is matchless. Lipkin lived an extraordinary life through extraordinary times and wrote the poems I've translated here about those events listed in the Chronology. In addition, it was he who helped to save Vasily Grossman's manuscript of *Life and Fate* from the KGB and took further personal risks to set it on course for publication in the West eleven years after Grossman's death. He is a poet revered throughout the former USSR, but virtually unknown in the West.

On this occasion, it has not been possible to produce a bilingual book; however, an appendix listing the original poems and where they can be found has been prepared. Further, and for clarity, the prose sections of this book were translated into US English, while the poems, some having been previously published in UK literary magazines and other publications, are reproduced in UK English.

Yvonne Green
December 2022
London

INTRODUCTION

Lipkin and Lisnyanskaya

Semyon Lipkin (1911–2003) and his wife Inna Lisnyanskaya (1928–2014) formed one of the most extraordinary couples in the history of Russian literature. As poets they never achieved the same international (or national) recognition as the greatest of their contemporaries – Pasternak, Tsvetaeva, Akhmatova, and Mandelstam – for they worked within existing traditions, rather than trying to break the mould. But as witnesses to the struggles of their contemporaries and to the fortunes of Russia under Stalin's terror, Nazi invasion and the post-Stalinist period of lies and suppression, Lipkin and Lisnyanskaya deserve the rank of martyrs, even though they were both vouchsafed a longevity extraordinary for a Russian poet in any era.

No Russian poet has written poetry over such a long period as Lipkin: his first poem appeared in 1926 when he was 15, his last shortly before his death in 2003. The thousand or so poems he wrote over those seventy-five years are all beautifully crafted, thoughtful and original. If he has never been ranked with Osip Mandelstam and Marina Tsvetaeva (both of whom patronised him, and were helped by him), it is because he deliberately aligned himself with poets such as Ivan Bunin: craftsmen, not magi; silver, rather than gold. Under Stalin, Lipkin remained, by some miracle, an honest intellectual and an observant Jew[1], seeking neither approval nor martyrdom. He was also an Orientalist, most admired as a translator of the Kyrgyz national epic, a modest career that became dangerous when Stalin in the late 1930s changed official encouragement of such national epics to condemnation of their 'nationalist' deviations. In the late 1920s, official Soviet policy encouraged the popularization of the culture of national minorities; under the Great Terror of 1937–8 such popularization suddenly became the crime of bourgeois nationalism. And towards the end of the Second

World War, in many cases, when a national minority, such as the Kalmyks or Crimean Tatars, had hoped for liberation by Hitler from Soviet rule, it became outright treason. Lipkin, unlike many translators of languages such as Kyrgyz, had a genuine competence in Central Asian Turkic: his gifts became a source of jeopardy, nearly as dangerous as his Jewishness, once Stalin took the anti-Semitic mantle over from Hitler.

After the fall of the USSR, Lipkin became better known. But his most widely read work has been not his verse but his *Kvadriga*, memoirs of his extraordinarily long and wide-ranging friendships: their humour and observation offset only by a certain puritanism. Nevertheless, Lipkin often reminds one of James Boswell: his visits to Akhmatova and his long friendship with Vasily Grossman are recorded with the same remarkable talent for verbatim recall and for nonjudgmental self-effacement. Like Boswell, Lipkin was pleased by any words of praise he received from his idols. Like Boswell, Lipkin played a vital role in immortalizing his collocutor. It is quite possible that, had Lipkin and Lisnyanskaya not succeeded in preserving a manuscript of Grossman's novel *Life and Fate* – arguably the most important work of fiction in twentieth-century Russia – it would have vanished into the cellars of the KGB.

Lipkin's political activism was quieter than Grossman's: he rarely fought for the right to publish a contentious work, and his and Lisnyanskaya's protests were expressed passively, for example by resignation from the Writers' Union. But he was troubled by the same official lie that tormented Grossman, Solzhenitsyn and other more or less dissident post-Stalinist writers: the Soviet authorities refused to recognize the Holocaust, portraying the death of millions of Soviet Jews as merely part of the martyrdom of the USSR, refusing to admit that the Gestapo and the NKVD, the Nazi and the Communist Parties were mirror images of each other, and limiting de-Stalinization to a slow programme of mean-minded 'rehabilitation' of some of Stalin's victims. Lipkin's poetry, not gathered in book form until the 1990s, is important as political testimony. Like his friend Grossman he dared to make the Holocaust his subject, and, like very few Russian poets, he mourned the premature deaths of those who returned, physically destroyed, from the GULAG.

Lipkin, like Grossman, wrote novels about Stalin's oppression. One of them, *Dekada*, is a thinly fictionalized account of Stalin's deportation in 1944 of the Balkar people from the North Caucasus, but their narrative and characterization are wooden. Only when he has the challenge of a metrical framework, as in 'The Technical Lieutenant-Quartermaster', can Lipkin release his full creative powers to deal with the conflicts and the chaos of world war. Other Lipkin poems also have the force of a politically motivated novel: his long 'Nestor and Saria', about the murder of Nestor Lakoba, the charismatic and humane leader of Soviet Abkhazia in the 1920s and early 1930s, by Lavrenti Beria on Stalin's orders, is of great interest because of undocumented information that Lipkin obtained, as well as because of its pathos, for the Lakoba marriage was a tragic version of Lipkin's and Lisnyanskaya's happy union. The poem may have limited aesthetic merit, but it completes the picture of Lipkin's civic courage.

Much longer and more productive than that of the Brownings, the marriage of Lipkin and Lisnyanskaya is almost unique in the history of literature. Lisnyanskaya's poetry stretches over forty years and, like Lipkin's, relies very much on the classical Russian tradition. Both poets incorporate into the metaphysical tradition of nineteenth-century Russian poetry, of Tiutchev and Baratynski, Jewish elements of *kaddish* and Old Testament legends. Lisnyanskaya often sounds (and her poetry was particularly effective when read aloud) as if she had reincarnated Anna Akhmatova, by re-enacting the feelings of the Biblical Ruth, Shulamith or Lot's wife. The role of the wife mourning the destruction of the city and the family became only too apt for Soviet women poets. The interaction of Lipkin and Lisnyanskaya in their defence of oppressed writers and in their exchange of lyrical poems is a subject for future investigation, and it will be much helped by Yvonne Green's pioneering work of selection and translation.

Donald Rayfield
London

ALEXANDER SOLZHENITSYN ON SEMYON IZRAILEVICH LIPKIN'S POEMS FROM *FREE WILL* (ARDIS PUBLISHING, 1981) IN *NOVY MIR* (MOSCOW, NO.4, 1998)

There was a bizarre phenomenon in the Soviet Union (and perhaps beyond it for various reasons); outstanding poets existed almost imperceptibly, noiselessly, in the literary world. They were little known for decades because they didn't rush to serve regimes, as nearly all other members of the poet côterie did.

Semyon Lipkin and his wife, Inna Lisnyanskaya, were part of this phenomenon. Lipkin was admitted to The Writers' Union as a young man on the strength of only a few uncollected publications. In order to save himself from the debasement of Soviet poetic life, he proceeded to translate poetry from Kalmyk, Kirghiz, Kabardian, and other Asian languages. He was then called up and became a war correspondent. After the war, he continued with his work as a translator, further immersing himself in oriental themes and philosophy.

In 1963 he conveyed his impressions of the front lines of 1941 in a very truthful epic, 'The Technical Lieutenant-Quartermaster', the publication of which was out of the question. However, by the end of the 1960s and throughout the 1970s, collections of Lipkin's poems appeared, the most comprehensive being published abroad when he was in his seventies.

Unsurprisingly, Lipkin's poems reflected how he was oppressed by the public silence forced on him; however, he "was cunning to the crowd" and "didn't tell the whole truth even to himself," but the years of isolation pinched and brought hopelessness, he wrote:

> …
>
> are we lost
> You, my poor verse, and I?

Have we joined a mute cooperative?"[2]

...

And tell Russia,

That only we are the living

And the Temple subsists[3]

After so much silence:

Speak about the cost of war

The sweet illusion that life's not begun,

Of how you are yet to be born.[4]

However, an axe looms even over the silent:

Terrified of prison ...[5]

who are threatened by the very people who reject the laws of man.

Stupidly I wait for fate

With only one insistent thought

That I must bury my fear well,

And my smile is ugly.[6]

The theme of prison camps and exile repeatedly breaks into his poems. Over and again, there's sympathy for exiles, and compassion for the convicted, in 'One of My Friends,' 'This and That,' 'The Taiga' as well as in 'Funeral' where he says:

The exhausted tundra, whitened by insults,

Beaten by hard labour, sobs, bleeds from old wounds,

Cries out from Russia's heart –

Dissident.[7]

And in 'Drawing Of A Greek Square', he describes the 'kurkuls'[8] distraught with hunger:

Who lay side by side ...

Unable to stand up or leave,

Lipkin's sympathy also extends to the Koreans exiled from

Primorye[9] to Central Asia.

He examines closely those who spent their whole lives creating the Gulag in 'Soldier of the Revolution,' 'The Executioner,' and 'Nestor and Saria.' In 'Solikamsk in August 1962' he also examines how the Gulag endured under Khrushchev. The accuracy of the description amazes me because I saw Kizel (which was near Solikamsk and belonged to the same camp system) a month before that poem was written. In that poem, Lipkin goes beyond mere description and asks what the victims would have done if they'd succeeded? Could they have become the executioners?

Lipkin's sympathy with the regime's victims often extends to the sharp pain of Russia's villages, 'Chastushka' is about how people secretly fled expropriation for over 5000 miles until they reached Asia, and 'Moonlight' is about city boys who:

> … use probes
> To look for bread from nightfall
> Until the Turkish sabre moon,
> Which lights up the peasant families,
> Pales over the steppe shacks,
> In red wagons
> They'll become insomniacs,
> Who'll mourn
> The distortion of truth –

He asks of the extinct village:

> Has the devil marked this hamlet?
> The cockerel's silent at dawn
> No one dreams or sobs among the limes,
> The milk churns don't rattle in the barns,
> There's just a long row of empty houses
> As silent as a shrouded corpse.[10]

Lipkin's heartfelt sympathy for the village extends to all of Russia:

> If I dig deep,
> In rot and mud
> Will I find the light
> Of all my Russia.[11]

His sense of war is informed by his experience as a soldier and in 1942 as a war correspondent, he drove in an editorial car through Cossack territory where villagers gloated over the Red Army's retreat, asking:

> Maybe you're Jews?

His poem's protagonist's reaction is:

> And what is strange, just then,
> As I see this land ungoverned,
> Just then,
> As I see it only at night,
> In the starless, primitive terror of night,
> Just then,
> When resignation
> Gives way to dark, hostile menace,
> Just then is when I first feel
> This territory is Russia,
> I am Russia,
> That without Russia, I'm nothing –
> And the joy of freedom –
> The crazy, drunk,
> Doomed-to-perish betrothal with death
> Penetrates me,
> Becomes me –
> I want to cry for this new happiness,
> And kiss the Cossack's cruel land –
> However cruel that land is to me.[12]

Here Lipkin reaches poetic heights, universals, transcends the national. A number of heartfelt poems with Christian Orthodox subjects follow: 'Beggars in 1922', 'In the Field Behind the Forest', 'On the Istra', 'When You Appeared To Me In My Native Town', and this theme naturally merges with Lipkin's religious contemplations and ecumenical dreams.

From the Russian North, Lipkin moves South to New Russia[13]. In 'Southern Churches' he responds warmly to its churches, which he describes as "little blue clay-walled huts," saying, "Their clothes don't shine," but of them, he says:

> … the heart buzzes
> With ancient tunes,
> The air of warm-heartedness.

During his life, Lipkin traveled widely in the Soviet Union, researching and empathizing with local culture and color. Time and again, he shows great sensitivity to the vast, multi-faceted East, often taking the Caucasus and Central Asia as his themes. He was well-informed and translated passionately, and taught himself the region's languages.

For all this, Lipkin's work retained its Jewish themes. He wrote of Odesa:

> And knowing nothing fresher
> Than the music of the interrogation in their accents
> The irony of their grammar
> Is unique[14]

He asks if it is:

> Painted by Chagall,

Or if it embodies:

> Lit by the Kabbalah's mystery[15]

In 'Commissar,' he described a young man called Joseph, who'd served in CheKa[16], then went on to be imprisoned in a camp. In 'The Taiga,' he describes the execution of trees by loggers and merges the tragedy of "the rigid blue of Russia's hungry villages" with the shooting of Jews at Babi Yar.

He addresses the Jewish Holocaust often, with respectful restraint, such as in 'Vilnius Compound', and with great force, in 'Ashes,' where the protagonist is burnt down, in his mother's uterus, in a state of lost consciousness, looking for the city he was born in:

> Charred and ashen I whisper *I've been cremated.*
>
> …
>
> I think *I'm blind confounded*
> *My palate has claimed my tongue.*
>
> …
>
> I ask *how do I find my way to Odesa?*
> Born burnt I can't yet mourn
>
> What it means to be alive or dead.
> My cold embers won't light a flame.

'Moses' consists of twelve lines[17] on the subject; unbearable tension accelerates in the first eight lines[18] until it is released skilfully in the poem's 'golden section', which introduces the regality of God.

Lipkin may be extremely thirsty for faith, but in 'Odesa Synagogue' he speaks of God's unattainability, saying[19]:

> I'm just a passerby
> But help me, God,
> Oh help!

He wrote a poem about a small tribe called 'Yi[20]'. Everyone realized it was about The Jewish State[21] [and the Jews], although a rumor[22] circulated that the small "Yi" tribe referred to in the poem was Chinese.

'Nomads' Fire' is another poem that addresses the intense spiritual search embodied in national consciousness:

> What is our destiny,
> When will there be rest from the chase?

Or are we the nomads' fire
Formless, eternal?

More than once, Lipkin delves into Old Testament motifs, sometimes conflating them with those of The Gospel:

… horror's knowledge
Penetrates the heart's dark bulk …
… Did we lie down there alone
Cry when the ground did? [23]

Lipkin's work is classical, in the main, unlike anything written today. His long poems such as 'At Joy's Summit', 'Literary Memoir' and 'Nestor and Saria' are cast, sculpted, traditional, and organic to the enduring continuum of the Russian canon.

Lipkin's stanzas are built with dense wording and paced with absolute ease of breath; he uses fresh (not hackneyed or forced) rhyme, of which Turgenev/sirenev, Lilov/lyubov are examples. He's not wedded to metaphor, but when he uses it, he does so with clarity:

Do we need the colour of a gypsy band
Verbal-carnival, contrivance,
Fists of fresh epithets

Or metaphors?:

… If only four of the lines
I write in my old age
Could become prayers
In our horrible world.[24]

Lipkin's compressions are rare but powerful; he speaks of Moldavian's "cart horse Latin[25]." His lines are sustained in high epic tone. His poems, plots, and content differ. Some are less concrete than others, but purity of soul, sincerity, and enduring nobility mark them all:

Can mankind live on earth

If even one, even the smallest tribe
Is missing?[26]

He says of animals:

A person of stature isn't noble,
If he's devoid of affinity for the lowly,
He's no right to freedom,
If his friend is chained.[27]

He says of trees:

… the rights of plants were abused …
Why do we make war against the forest's tribes,
For books, watchtowers – do gas ovens
Need firewood? Why do we execute trees …?[28]

Dried out walnuts and poplars have destiny to contend with:

The pine, the oak
Have endless ways to suffer
But not one to describe suffering.[29]

He is particularly sensitive to trees, their "barely perceptible whisper" their species, Northern, Southern, whether pine, acacia, cypress, even the individual character of each of their trunks; he is sensitive to all vegetation, everything that grows.[30]
He discerns:

… the language of the grass
more complex than poems or chess.[31]

He emphasizes the grandeur of water that "thunders and fulminates"[32], describes the drinking of "stagnant [desert] water.[33]"
He discerns the character of each wave in the sea[34], each bird, grasshopper, and blade of grass. He engages in a "wordless conversation" with the monads of nature, reads "cuneiform in plants," converses with the living hieroglyphs of matter.[35]
Lipkin's sense of the world is deeply pantheistic without

singling out any particular religion; he shows deep interest in and sympathy with all of them. He sees everywhere the grains of beauty in human suffering, lived with the strange knowledge that there is truth in the world, fundamental, unearthly, that even human sorrow celebrates life, expresses being:

> I found joy in repentance and my weakness gave me
> Strength.[36]

Most of Lipkin's poetry is philosophically significant, examines the very root of human existence, and engages with transcendent philosophical concepts; examples are, 'Tao,' 'Time,' 'The Monkey-House,' 'When Forgetting The Concepts Of Early Days.'

Another of Lipkin's motifs is the unity of mankind's existence, the continuum with those who have lived long before us:

> But the living and those who've lived
> We're all close. What's the past?
>
> … Death is something we won't pass,
> Time is what's dead in memory.
>
> And more than once I've been surprised
> By how nothing's divided from us by years;
> The Angel in The Apocalypse swore
> That time would disappear forever.[37]

Lipkin's 'At Joy's Summit' is a strange, dualistic, philosophical poem that doesn't address religious feeling. However, 'Conversation' and 'Two Nights' are poems in which Lipkin's philosophical reflection rises to the religious as surely as when he asserts:

> But the roar of the Last Judgment
> We will not forget, we will not forget …[38]

Lipkin writes with unforgettable and aphoristic concision:

> The collapse of a heart
> More frightening than a split atom.

To discern
The direct power of truisms
And the round seal of falsehood.

Only life is a requital,
And death the horror of it.

The way to luck,
Is timely death.

The anxious burn of the afterthought
That you haven't done much good, is good.

ENDNOTES

1   Lipkin was an observant Jew and a zionist who visited Israel with Lisnyanskaya who later retired there with her family after she was widowed.

2   'The Cooperative Of Deaf Mutes'.

3   'Ghosts'.

4   'In No Faith, Freedom, Love'.

5   'I Bought You My Thoughts'.

6   'Early Summer'.

7   Denotes the offense created by the fifty eighth article of the Russian Penal Code, being. conduct or propaganda deemed to be anti-Soviet.

8   A synonym of "kulak", the Soviet term (meaning "fist") which denoted peasants alleged to be wealthy which the Soviet regime persecuted.

9   The Far-Eastern part of the USSR.

10   A Hamlet'.

11   'A Nook In The Forest'.

12   'The Technical Lieutenant-Quartermaster'

13   Novorossiya – the area north of the Black Sea which was conquered by Tsarist Russia at the end of the 18th Century which included Odesa where Lipkin was born..

14   'Autumn At The Sea'.

15   'May Night In The Forest'

16   Name of Soviet repressive secret police in the first years of Communist power in Russia.

17   Ten in our translated version.

18   Six in our translated version.

19   In our translated version..

20   The extended monosllyable "yi" in Russian translates as "and".

21   "Yi" is the first syllable of the country name, Israel, in Russian.

22   Lipkin told Sergei Makarov that he'd started this false rumour.

23   'I Hear Them Carrying Sand From The Sandpit'.

24   'Do We Need The Colour Of A Gypsy Band'

25   'Moldavian is a Language'.

26   'The Technical Lieutenant-Quartermaster'.

27   'Dogs'.

28   'The Taiga'.

29   'The Silent'.

30   'Sunday Morning In The Forest'.

31   'Fantasy'

32   'Thrush'

33   'In The Desert'

34   'By The Sea'

35   'In The Daytime'.

36   'When I Was Putting Letters Into Words' ('I Was Accompanied By A Crazy Century').

37   'Time'.

38   'Storm'

.

ENGLISH VERSIONS OF THE POEMS CITED BY ALEXANDER SOLZHENITSYN

The Technical Lieutenant-Quartermaster[1]

1

Krasnodar's bread is light,
Fresh, so white, it shocks me,
The kolkhoz[2] stocks its market
High and cheap so I don't need
The Commandant's coupons to buy
Baked milk and cheese from the Caucasus,
To reach into bins of dried fruit,
To choose bottles of cheap, mischievous, cloudy
Local wine, as red as the blood on the blade
Of a Cossack's shashka.[3]
Zinc-topped tables heave with glowing lard, giblets,
And preserved watermelons the housewives
Soaked in salt water for this, the first spring of the war.

I'm a lucky young lieutenant-quartermaster,
War's got rid of disease,
And as my father would have sung,
There are opportunities to seize.
I shaved in my truck's rear view mirror today,
My gymnastyorka[4] pocket is full of money,
The division's chief finance officer has paid me
Four months' in advance.
I'm groomed, lucky, bright, alive,
I know how to deal with the top brass,
And how handsome I look ruddied by the steppe.

I've found five trucks for my division in three days.
With a week to spare, there's time to have fun.
My paperwork's in order and it's spring in Krasnodar.
My trucks are lined up outside my billet,
The shine of their uneven, new, khaki paint job,
Brings respect to the master

Of this blue-washed, clay-walled house,
(So typical of the region), where Pomazan's relatives live.
And my old dust-browned, war-battered truck,
A splinter of the steppe, stands here
In the courtyard under a broad chestnut tree.
The drivers sleep in its cabin, on their pea-green jackets
When they get home from the women at dawn,
While I've slept here on the verandah with Pomazan,
Like a god, on my hosts' fresh sheets,
Satiated with bazaar food and drink,
Excited by this Spring,
In a city with boulevards and wine,
No saddle under me, no enemy in front,
No commander above, no wormwood or feather grass around.
Drunk on the moment,
I jump carefully off the open platform of my tram,
Stand still, then with nothing better to do,
Go into a shop with books, pads, grey wrapping paper,
Rulers and pencil cases on the shelves.
A slattern in lipstick rebuffs me from the till,
If you want dominos and cards you have to pre-order –
Dejected I look at the books,
Remember I love words,
And buy a Polish-Russian dictionary on impulse.

Do you have interest to learn Polish?
Someone says – neither his jacket,
Syntax, or accent are Russian,
The dome of his bald patch descends steeply onto his eyebrows,
Which are as heavy and black as an Assyrian king's,
The flames of Shtetl confusion burn in his sunken eyes,
His hooked nose peels, his cheeks are unshaven,
He reeks of leather,
Horse sweat, wine, garlic, manure.
We leave together, my new acquaintance and I,

He was a lawyer in Poland, now he's a guard in a Sovkhoz[5]
Near town, over there, on the other side of the river.
He's so happy to know me – he studied in Warsaw and Vienna –
Was a communist, then a member of Poalei Zion,[6]
Now he's a keen Tolstoyan.
He gesticulates, susurrates[7] freely
(I noticed long ago that everyone susurrates in their own way),
He confuses dialects, shouts names in my ears,
Kautsky, Gandhi, Böhm-Bawerk, Freud, Bergson.

Suspiciously frank,
He says he's shocked
By the illogicality of our regime,
Its brutal hangman's innocence,
Our truly strong Sovereign Leader
Is like an African Chief, he says,
He's as fierce, frightening, false and weak as an actor,
Isn't it also strange that the State proclaims
Soviet Man triumphant,
Brave, kind, clever, strong and beautiful,
Meanwhile State institutions,
Whether parks, post offices or grocers
Treat you like a thief or a fool,
Riddled with vice?
He's so excited to find me,
Of the chance to speak out,
He's been in dialogue with himself
For so long. But talking to this
Internee scares me more than German tanks,
With his sunken eyes which blaze like Isaiah's,
His crazy talk,
So I leave him, abruptly, without warning,
Walk off, abandon him among the spring crowds.
An illogical affront to him.
But since I'm not just a coward,

But also a human being,
I turn around at the corner,
Feel my eyes plead for forgiveness.
And he, a fallen leaf hurled out
Of the European wood by the total whirlwind of 1939
To a Kuban Sofkhoz, stands and looks at me without malice,
Furrows his Assyrian eyebrows.

And suddenly, with an uncharacteristic premonition,
Probably borrowed from his Isaiah eyes, I see
Hot summer approach, my division scattered
On horseback, on foot, lost,
Rushing between Sal'sk and Armavir,
The steppe's black, a crescent moon hangs over the melon fields
Which look as though they're spattered with blood.
The lizards, crickets, leaves and birds, are all worked up,
They can't to go to sleep that night, so they talk and talk
About the human war, but the humans themselves are silent,
Their horses are silent, somewhere in the distance
Bullets flash – or are they cigarettes, falling stars?
A handful of riders appear
Led by a fat bow-legged old Kalmyk Colonel
With a clay-smooth face –
He's a good soldier, a hero of the Civil War
Who's tired of it all, the constant retreats,
His long army service with its slow poison of disappointments,
All the nights without sleep – lack of man-to-man combat,
The Germans' magic supremacy,
No leave
No loyalty from Kurtz, his Commissar,
Who's clever but an enthusiastic informer …
Where you going, Pan[8] Officers, gentlemen?
The Germans are here!
A horseman screams, as he suddenly appears
Out of the dark cut off from it by the half moon,

Barefoot, in cotton pants and vest, on an unsaddled horse,
A strap in his hand, in a world where all heads are protected
With the military might of sweaty caps,
His bald head looks naked, feeble.
Pan officer!, the Colonel echoes,
In a hoarse imperious voice, *Sabre him, he's German!*
He doesn't know that it's only my acquaintance from Krasnodar,
Who's again been swept up in a plague-ridden storm,
Together with his Sovkhoz, and his confusion,
But the experienced Kurtz understands, fortunately,
Jokes, nervously, *If only all Germans were like him!*
He's from Berdichev, he's one of us.

Is the end near?
How long will the lawyer from Warsaw
Rush about with Rambouillet sheep on the southern steppe?
Will they grab him, turn him into ashes,
Or is he destined for another death?
Will the handful of riders meet with others,
The old Kalmyk, the Colonel with a god's clay face,
Who's served in the ranks for 25 years,
Was a Sergeant-Major under Kerensky.
What does this Colonel understand about this war?
Will he be brave, wise, use skill to fight,
Break out of the encirclement?
And if he does, what for?
So that one night in 1944 his ancient people
Can be evicted from the steppe? Oh Lieutenant-Quartermaster,
Lieutenant-Quartermaster, what did you understand back then?
You hadn't seen anything of the world yet but yourself.

2

I'm sitting on a bench in a shaded square – it's not ideal,
It's the avenue where the Front's headquartered,
The top brass come and go, they'd retreated too quickly

And shamefully from the Crimea, now they're so crisp,
Efficient, important. The women sergeants make me feel shy
As they sashay past me with their permanent waves
And their dresses, sewn for them in the Generals' tailor shops.
Then I hear, *Hey, Lieutenant-Quartermaster, getting a nice tan?*
I am addressing you, my brothers and sisters.[9]

I raise my head and see Zadnepruk,
A forty-year-old Lieutenant, who's been hanging about for ages
With no appointment at my Cavalry Division –
He's got brown cheeks, small sharp eyes,
His upper lip's turned inside out by an old war wound,
His coarse crew-cut hair's sprinkled with the grey salt
Of Solikamk's gulag, his shoulders are broad as an oven,
Muscles straining against the fabric of his blue jacket,
And he wears a single new medal on the bell of his chest
For 20 Years Continuous Service to the Red Army[10].
There's nothing to do here in town except
Loaf about and twiddle your thumbs –
Here on business? Obviously …
He both asks then answers for me and sits down.
Words pop out of his disfigured mouth like bullets,
They hiss, sharp, *I was up before the Front Party Commission –*
Rehabilitated by the honour and conscience of the epoch.[11] *–*
Don't think it was simple. I managed to get in to see the Chief –
He remembered me right away – from the First Cavalry Army –
He told me he thought his head would roll too,
Or he'd be sent on a one-way trip like I was
To polish bears' horseshoes –
The Chief said Great Stalin used to call me and Oka over[12] *–*
Mind you he was Marshal and Colonel-General –
We had to sing and dance for him –
It's not that we were acting, we were just loyal to him,
But in my mind, you know, there were other dances –
Then the Chief asks me, Have you got a girl? No?

Find yourself one of the female medics and get going!
You'll soon be a Major with a regiment of your own!
Zadnepruk says, *You can leave,*
But I'll stay here for a couple of days first.
My personal life's dismal,
I need some rest and relaxation –
Could you spare me five hundred rubles?
We separate, not knowing
We'll need each other soon.
With a whole week free
I go down the evening street
With no goal, past the boat yard
To the Kuban river which groans wistfully
As if it runs over a forge,
Seethes so loud,
That the whole earth seems implicated in its blood feud,
Dashes to its shores with such anger and violence
That when you look down from its steep banks
Its water swirls like time
And time runs like a rabid river,
You can't tell by its upper reaches what its lowlands are.
It's spring, my time's ahead,
My time's in the steppe, in the July steppe,
Surrounded by the enemy.

    3

What can I see at the bottom of the turbulent river of time,
What can I see from the slits in the observation point
To where I've been sent by the Chief of Staff?
I see a Don meadow,
A wood on the hill, a stretch of water
Which the trees climb out of like drunken men,
And next to them, a foal,
Born three months ago, emerges as if on tiptoe,
And presses its muzzle down to its pasterns.

Down in the trench, a fresh slogan
Is pinned by the weeds to the crumbling wall,
The Germans will not pass through the Don –
On the other side, bombs explode in the mornings
And rockets flare at night.
People come in thin and black with dust
They plod weary from the bundles they shoulder,
Like miners from the town of Shakhta,
At the river's crossing there's chaos,
A great resettlement of citizens,
A great migration of livestock,
A great military retreat,
Everyone wants to board the ferry
Which our modest division operates.
Everyone's on the run.

A Lieutenant wanders into a shed,
Starts shooting in the air with his Parabellum[13].
His documents check out,
I'm the pompotekh[14] of an artillery battalion
I've lost my unit,
He says and smiles shyly,
I've come from Millerovo to Stalingrad.
When he's asked, *Why were you shooting?*
He answers, *Because.*

In the Don morning
The east wind from the Kalmyk steppe
Breathes with the sand where feather-grass grows,
In bitter-salt earth, scorched heat, pressed dung smoke
Old life, hung over from drinking koumiss,
Sound like four kinds of cattle, lowing,
Like the call of nomads moving camp.
And the west wind
Gentle, soft, flies in from the great,

Served, pampered, civilized, world,
It hurts when it stops as abruptly
As the whistle of a shunting locomotive.

Oh, Lieutenant-Quartermaster, Lieutenant-Quartermaster,
Do you know now the way a cavalry division's wild retreat begins?
They shoot on the river bank, in the cherry orchards,
At the Headquarters, Political Department, and village councils,
Phones ring, sleepily as if they don't believe in themselves.
From the posts where they're hitched, Cossack horses
Look into open windows with a kind of smirk
At clerks, at notice boards hung with propaganda –
You laugh too early, you war horses, too early –

It's quiet and dusty, the day is long, hot –
The Chemical Squadron Commander
Teaches himself how to ride,
Our newspaper editor's anxious,
He was promised calfskin boots, his car,
Covered with a black tarpaulin, stands
On the verge of a farmstead which edges the steppe
At the very rear of the fighting division,
And the steppe's as alive as an animal,
Its puddles stone-grey, its grass flame-red,
Its serene-faced Cossack girls
Washing foul underwear in the very river –
That's the front line –
The steppe pours into the sky
Just like the soul forces
Life's beauty into the body,
As rough as life and as beautiful –

Tanks, tanks – we're surrounded –
Screams a lost horseman out of nowhere, then disappears
And there, in the east, where the steppe pours into the sky,

Unexpected, the way submarines surface,
Dark, almost static monsters appear,
The land breaks loose, runs,
And what it had been made of,
Houses, barns, crops, meadows, gardens –
Merge into a single entity, which spins,
And the division breaks loose, runs.
What had seemed like a single entity,
Subject to laws,
Gravity,
Breaks down into parts
Not squadrons, regiments, headquarters, command posts,
Officers, Commissars, State,
The soldier disappears, the civilian's born,
And he runs for his life –
Even the roughest, bravest, most ingenious
Commander's brutality can't stop the retreat,
Because now, terrified,
Trenchant, hopeful,
Civilians, not soldiers, gallop on horseback,
In all directions,
Some away from the Germans, some towards them,
There are horseless riders and riderless horses too,
They pant as they run in the dust,
The man who raised the alarm,
Who panics most of all,
Turns out to be Obnosov,
Who everyone fears,
That Captain with a broad face,
He looks huge now,
All his features are marooned,
In the middle of his face,
Surrounded by his endless white flesh,
It turns out that this dreaded NKVD Captain, Obnosov,
Has a woman's body, and it's flabby,

Turns out he cries like a woman over the safe
That holds the greatest asset of the State's Power –
The testimony of agents who've denounced
The actions of the Division's staff, cadres,
Because staff, cadres, as the Leader's taught us, decide everything.[15]

    4

For Motherland! For Stalin!
The Commander of the bled-out squadron screams,
After it fights to the death in cherry orchards,
Rushes to the steppe to meet armoured vehicles –
Remember him: Tseren Pyurbeev,
Our best comrade fighter,
The darkest-faced of the division
With the whitest teeth,
The cleanest undercollars,
The roundest cheekbones,
The jaw hinged under a film of sunburn,
Small, in his stiff felt cloak,
Who sits high on his horse?
He wields an anti-tank gun now,
Fires it –
He's ashamed of us, himself, his tribe,
The milk of his mother's sweat.
He wants to believe he'll rally the troops
But they just run. And I watch gripped,
See Pyurbeev's head, in his yellow field cap,
Bounce off his black felt cloak,
His horse flinches.
His cloak stays in the saddle –
Time, what are you, a moment, eternity?
Tribe, what are you, an element, everything?
This morning, in the kibitka[16], Pyurbeev's sister, Nina,
Read the triangle[17] they'd received from Tseren
To her illiterate father.

This sick man plucked his beard,
Nodded in time
To his son's letter's music, elegance, courtesy –
Now his son's head rolls on the grass of the Don steppe.
And on the last night of 1943 – New Year's eve,
Pyurbeev's sister, all the Ulus, every Kalmyk tribe
Will be taken, first by car, then cattle train, to Siberia –
Can the Don steppe's grass survive when the last are gone,
Can mankind live on earth
If even one, even the smallest tribe
Is missing?
But what do I, Lieutenant-Quartermaster, know about this?
I'm washed by time, like a river washes rock around its flows
I'll stay alive, stand,
But not like I do now, stunned by the retreat, its insanity,
I'll stand anxious, expectant,
In front of the samovar
At a burnt out station near Stalingrad,
On a dirty winter's morning.
Watched by long, steel-grey eyes
Which look out from the narrow prison windows
Of the box-car of a strange train, under army escort,
Eyes which plead like those of old horses
Loaded into huge slaughterhouse lorries,
Eyes which look like earth's sadness,
Old as time,
Endless as the steppe –

Maybe Tseren's sister
Nina Pyurbeev,
Will be one of them.
She was so modern
So neat, with her long braids,
So trim – a teacher,
With solid notions of love,

Syntax, culture.
She'll be allowed one suitcase,
She'll take the certificate which attests
To her brother's posthumous Hero's Star,
A Buddhist folk epic – illustrated,
The well known Russian edition,
Linen and Clothes,
A brick of tea
But not even the smallest piece of bread
To deceive a starved stomach,
Nor blade of grass, nor gopher,
If her parents had still been alive,
They'd have thrown a gopher into the pot.

Maybe the fat, round, strong,
Fleshy-buttocked, gold-toothed, mother of four,
Trade unionist head,
Tegryash Bimbaeva will be there,
Married to a traitor – a policeman
Who'd run off with the Germans,
She knows she'll be deported, she'll be ready,
With cases of foreign tinned food[18],
She'll offer sausages and soups with love, one to a friend,
Who won't take them, she'll offer them to Nina,
Who wont' take them,
Take them, take them! the old women will shout,
We're one tribe, one blood! –
But Nina won't,
Take them, take them!
The flat-chested young women will shout,
Is she to blame for her husband?
Why do you stand still, Lieutenant-Quartermaster,
(Though, by then you'll be a Captain),
Do you see this box car,
Hear the shouting,

Will you stop the train which exiles the tribe?
Killing any tribe, even a small one,
Is the shameful end of humanity,
Stop the train, stop the train,
If you don't you're guilty, you, you're to blame.

Hey, are you mad – trying to get to the enemy?
They're waiting for you with open arms!
Quick, jump into this car –
I hear Major Zadnepruk's voice,
His regiment's crumbled like sand,
Like the sand of the steppe,
I hear the hiss of his voice from up on his horse,
From the swirl of grass and retreat,
And suddenly I'm in the editor's van
Knocking the peak of my cap on the amerikanka's[19] lever.'
The typesetters and superannuated soldiers,
Stop letter-sets bouncing out of their cases.
And surprise of surprises, Pomazan's the driver
Of this retreating van
Through whose windows, cut in black canvas,
Zadnepruk suddenly appears
Waving commands with his free hand,
And in a dip, under the sharp-leafed willow,
Meek in his last sleep
There's a tiny foal, probably the same foal
Who at dawn, tiptoed out of the Don.

5

Pomazan still doesn't know anything about this,
He's still with me on my trip after I found the trucks,
He still snores next to me on his relatives' veranda,
The spring night is still coal black,
I still feel a smirk,
When I remember Zadnepruk saying,

My personal life's completely down in the dumps.
I'm looking forward
To a pleasant adventure in Krasnodar,
Already in front of me shines
A girl's tired, young face,
Made beautiful by the pain of separation,
There are forbidden tears in her wide eyes,
Her hair loose on her shoulders,
Hands that tremble, her endless prattle.

Suddenly at the end of deceitful March,
When the air's heavy with damp and cold,
The steppe gives birth
To waves of young, sharp, desperate heat,
Ghostly Mayan castles from South India
Reflect out of the pure gold of its mirages
In puddles as wide as lakes,
And my new division
Rallies from the remnant
Of one of winter's raids,
When riders' life spans were as short as moths.
We move with ordinance and supplies,
Like a migrant tribe
Closer to the fire of war.

And I'm ordered ahead
With other Quartermasters,
To find lodgings and stables
In the village, for the Company and their horses,
(Only the Commander knows how long we'll be here),
Billets, as always, are assigned with care,
Headquarters and Political Department to the school,
Commissar Kurtz to the house of the Headmistress,
A neat and insightful woman in glasses,
Who wears earrings and pendants,

The Colonel, our Commander
To the kolkhoz chairman's comfortable house
Replete with pickles, jams and liqueur bottles,
Obnosov, the NKVD man
To the Party Secretary's house,
And the Chief of Staff,
Who everything depends on,
(Both in this world and the next),
Is assigned a room at the doctor's …

I ride the mare Biryuza,
Through the village, move as cautiously as a hunter,
See an unforgettable face
At a window –
Do I know that I'll never forget it?
When I tether Biryuza,
When six-year-old blond Sashka opens the door
His calico shirt untucked,
When I walk into the sitting room,
Which is long, cool and clean,
When I see that young, dark, part-gypsy face,
That shines, eager, shy, confident, confused,
When I hear that voice laugh, tremble, defy, mourn, question,
Maybe it won't be good enough here – for what you want?
Do I think then, that that voice, those eyes,
Will always stay in my heart?
I want to judge her when she chooses,
To come to me at night,
To whisper, *sweet, desired …*
Shouldn't have met you …
Place in my heart …
To speak about her husband, a mechanic,
Who hasn't written from the front,
Strong, solid, not bad when he's sober –
When she says she's guilty before us both,

I want to judge her but can't,
Because she brings me,
A silly Lieutenant-Quartermaster,
To my fate, my love.

When I ride away from her house
At the end of the week,
She isn't ashamed in front of her village or the army,
She calls out, yells,
Strokes and kisses my clumsy hand,
While Sashka, for some reason, bawls and howls
So much, I'm relieved to get away.

    6

But slowly this changes,
And my soul begins to weigh heavy with sharp need.
Nine mornings after I leave,
Fiery mist rises over the water,
I watch it from what the locals call an exit route,
The cellar of a ruined house,
But I see no way out.
Just yesterday we numbered five hundred or so,
By morning there were only twenty-four of us left.
Five hundred of us were stopped
By the Zagradotryad[20] the previous day,
The retreat was routed
Not far from Palagiada's station,
Stalin's decree was declaimed,
It's Cossacks' rule all around here,
This territory has been ideologically tainted,
The Southern Front Armies are demoralized,
Stern measures and penal troops are what's needed,
Only blood can redeem your shame –"
The Colonel, as rotund as ever,
Cheers up and urges us to stand strong.

There is a lightning-fast battle
Fists against tanks, as our editor put it (he was killed yesterday), –
And my company again scatters in all directions,
Two of the Zagradotryad's come with me,
We run together,
And I keep asking, *Where are the squadrons –*
The Colonel – The Commissar – The Headquarters –
Horses – machine-gun carriers – trucks?
How did I end up in a cellar
With eighteen men and three sergeants,
And we three officers – myself,
Captain Obnosov – like a ghost with his precious safe –
And Zadnepruk?

I remember yesterday's retreat, it's vague, –
Vague – I don't understand –
What did we defend, when we defended –
With the Germans left, right, behind, in front –
We all dived into fresh, unknown trenches –
The armed, the unarmed
We all fired on command,
Except Obnosov and his groom,
Who sat in a machine-gun cart in a distant hollow
Guarding the safe.
I couldn't understand
Why the noble oak hung with cables
Flew into the air,
I couldn't understand
Where I should go –
Yesterday we'd been an army in retreat,
Now I'm part of the wind and dust –
I imagine that across the water
Orders aren't being given in Russian,
But here, beside me,
The corn still speaks Russian,

Begs silently for the harvest,
In the red sunset – the sky
As dark and smoke-filled
As a Russian village blacksmith's –
I wait for nightfall, then go,
Go straight to my own people.
Why do I go
Only when the day's over,
After the enemy invaded?
The captured territory's huge,
There aren't enough Germans
To control it.
There are ungoverned villages, hamlets,
It's a kind of miracle,
An ungoverned country,
Fields without authorities,
Without German authority, without our own,
People without authority,
Nights, one, two, even three, without authority.
Waking up in the morning,
The dewy leaves seem to tremble,
No authority – ungoverned.

We sleep during the day – in barns, sheds, fields of maize,
In the evening, one of us goes to ask the villagers,
When did our people leave here?
Who are your people? comes the question.
The Red Army.
So it is not ours but yours?
Ours is Russian, we specify, wising up,
That's not ours either.
Aren't you Russian? We ask,
No. We're Cossacks, one says,
Then, with a sneer and flint-sharp eyes, he asks,
Maybe you're Jews?

And what is strange, just then,
As I see this land ungoverned,
Just then,
As I see it only at night,
In the starless, primitive, terror of night,
Just then,
When resignation
Gives way to dark, hostile, menace,
Just then is when I first feel
This territory is Russia,
I am Russia,
That without Russia I am nothing,
And the joy of freedom –
The crazy, drunk,
Doomed-to-perish betrothal with death –
Penetrates me,
Becomes me.
I want to cry from this new happiness,
And kiss the Cossacks' cruel land –
However cruel that land is to me.

7

Obnosov comes to read a charge,
While we're hiding in a hut
On the Mozdok steppe, beyond the Don.
For some reason Zadnepruk hasn't folded back
His one-inch scaled map to our new location yet,
I've been informed, says Obnosov
That Pomazan burnt his party card yesterday,
Sergeant Larichev from the three hundred and thirteenth regiment,
Who watched Pomazan on my orders,
Saw him do it,
There were signs before –
I suggest we assemble the squadron tonight,
You, Comrade Major, will let everyone know,

Then Pomazan will be shot.
Listen, Obnosov, Zadnepruk hisses and swears,
Let's do it later
When we're back with our own people –
Obnosov, you're impossible, by God,
And you're as much use to the army
As a saddle sore

How dare you, blanches Obnosov,
His lips tremble, and his pale blue eyes flash,
Behind his market-doll's cheap glasses,
His doughy face contorts with pain,
I've never seen him look so human,
A saddle sore?
What are you without me?
Cowards, traitors to the Motherland, deserters –
And you Commander –
Accused under article fifty-eight, paragraph eleven,
Given the technical benefit of the court's doubt, but still …
That encirclement? That was no accident!
The Division's banner's in my safe –
A round seal, Comrade Major.
With me here, you're a military unit.
And who are you without me?
It hurts to hear all of this –
I don't deserve this from you,
Comrade Major – I address this to you,
Not as my commander but as Communist to Communist.

Calm down, Obnosov, Zadnepruk says,
He's quieter, conciliatory,
But I see his confusion,
I'm four years behind politically,
No great talker,
Don't worry, we'll shoot him –

After Obnosov leaves the branch's shelter,
Where we hid from the invaders,
Zadnepruk glares at me and says,
Pomazan's your friend –
You were with him at Krasnodar
Weren't you? Talk to him.

And I do,
I tell him everything, say, *Run –*
We are dirty, louse-infested,
Lying side by side in the green maize
Which spreads the spears of its leaves over us
Like swords of Damocles,
The early sun warms our backs,
The ground wets our hungry stomachs,
And it's here I learn
That Pomazan isn't Pomazan but Tereshko,
That his family were Ukrainian,
That his father had been wealthy,
That they'd all been exiled to Semirechye
As members of an alien class, in 1930
Dropped on the station platform
At the end of a single-track, steppe railway line –
A station called Divnoye[21] – *Don't you know it?* he asks,
It's not far he says,
In these arid, dry, windy places
Everywhere has names like that,
Divnoye, Priyutnoe[22], Izobil'noye[23].
There were commandants' offices everywhere
And once a day, from Petrovsky,
The train would pull up at the platform,
Like a snake at the gates of paradise,
With a kind hiss of steam from the locomotive
And everyone,
(Including the thirteen year old Tereshko,

His stomach bloated),
Dashed with all kind of cans,
To the engine, to the rail cars, to find water,
And from the best rail car
The worst water dripped
And they drank from the toilets there too,
Tereshko's mother, brother and two sisters died
And just like I say now,
His father said, *Run,*
Run, my boy, before you die.
And he ran, ran far away,
Mastered a trade
Married a waitress,
Took her surname,
Moved closer to the steppe
Through her,
Became a driver in Sarepta,
Upped the gears,
Was accepted into the Party,
Almost a joke: a teetotal driver,
Humble, hardworking,
A good mechanic,
Was discreet if he made illicit trips,
Gave the traffic superintendent his share.

And when I'm sent from the Division
For the lorries to Krasnodar,
Pomazan takes me and my fellow drivers
Not just anywhere, but to his father's house,
To his father, who'd married a tall, lean Baptist woman,
Silent as a shadow,
Who'd also been exiled to Divnoye.
They'd had new children,
In this new house Pomazan didn't know,
Pomazan's father's hair is grey,

But his skin is as brown as a boy's,
He works central stores,
Wholesale,
Is wealthy again.
I didn't hear Pomazan's father wake him
When I slept on the veranda,
I didn't hear him
Put a quart of his home brew on the table,
And weep to his teetotal son,
Drink, my boy, drink Styopa[24],
You came in the end, you came-
To see your old father
Styopa was Pomazan's dead brother's name.

And that evening, one of our men
Crawls a whole kilometre
To a pen and steals a sheep,
No one stands guard any more.
I'm happy to light a fire,
The fresh meat tastes good,
With fresh watermelon
We pick ourselves from the field,
I murmur to Zadnepruk as we eat,
A feast –
Fool, he says,
As he bites meat
Off the tip of his sabre,
And I suddenly notice that Obnosov's staring.

That night we all go east to the dark steppe
Flooded with foreign troops and disturbance
That only Zadnepruk understands,
A dog howls from somewhere, not a danger,
The distant sound of German orders seems worse
But something moves beside, around, within me,

And that seems the worst of dangers
And the far and the close merge and become fear.

We advance, know each other,
By the sound of our breath,
Sergeant Larichev, then Obnosov's orderly,
Shoulders the safe,
We stop, then start
In the hostile dark
The huge night closes its tired eyelids,
Mutters in a sick dream,
Wakes up, with sudden screamed terror,
What was that cry?
Only twenty-two of us see morning,
Obnosov and Pomazan are gone
And Larichev,
Sergeant to what remains of 313th,
Stammers, childlike,
Pomazan killed the Captain then ran –
But I know who killed the NKVD man,
With bitter joy, fear and awe
I glance at Zadnepruk's sabre,
Hidden in its chipped sheath,
As he yells, *Open it up, quick*!
And Larichev helps us open the safe –
Denunciations, dossiers, messages,
Some foxed, some fresh,
Spin, scatter, circle the steppe,
But some things stay inside the safe,
The red banner, our Cavalry Division's round seal.
Zadnepruk takes the banner out,
Folds it slowly, pockets it, then takes the seal,
And says, *Do you feel safer now, Larichev*?
Larichev is silent, it is a bad silence.
I think Pomazan is done with the war,

Know everyone feels the same.
Maybe I too should run away,
To the clean, sweet, well-fed village,
Where my Cossack woman lives,
Where I can pass for an Armenian,
No German could tell.
She loves me, would hide me,
Keep my secret …
But that night I get up and go east again
We all do,
Some without belts or shoes, but all with weapons,
We meet a stranded soldier
With faded eyes, hair, tunic, insignia,
Of whom we ask, *Where's our army … any news?*
Kazakhstan, he says, *maybe further*
How close are the Germans?
Tbilisi, he says, *they've brought the Georgians a King.*
We ask, *Where are you going?*
He answers, *To the front line to singe my eyebrows,*
To hell with that, we say, *want to come with us?*
He says, *I'll come if you'll have me.*

   8

Sand, sand –
Who said time flows like water?
Time flows like sand,
And sand smothers
The rare shrubs of meadow-sweet,
The smell of sage,
The stubborn roots of saltbushes,
The crystal shards of salty lakes.
And like time,
Sand can become a fool,
Rear like waves,
Rush like rivers,

Grind like mill wheels,
Swirl like water in a gust,
Cyclone into towered cities
Whose pink walks and turquoise domes
Fill half the sky.
Sand cheats,
With ghosts, shadows and haze.
Visions,
On the dry scorched plain
Of a runaway slave
Riding a horse he stole from a settlement,
A thirsty runaway
In the middle of the steppe,
The empty, dry, desert of a steppe,
A runaway who pierces his horse's vein,
Inserts a corn stalk,
Sucks out thick, warm blood –
Can blood quench thirst?
Horse and rider die,
The dead are swept away by the sand,
The steppes' sand.

Visions of one grain of sand,
Which speaks to another,
says, *We're of one blood – you and I*
Everyone else is different from us,
So let's strangle the rush of water,
Strangle what grows on earth,
Survive alone,
The steppes' sand.

But we don't give up
We, where the future starts,
And the future is retribution
Because one man and the next are the same

And no one else is his superior,
Because love's born even from evil,
And we men are the children of love.
So we cleave to one another
Not because we have the same blood,
But because we have the same love.

You might think that days merge
But actually they replace each other,
Time's reborn,
The day comes,
Which will blossom for me in Germany,
Where I'll ride with Zadnepruk
Along narrow streets with their bombed pavements,
Past the steps of a defiled church,
Between the houses with pitched roofs,
Where even the trees, air, gas stations
Are called to testify,
Not in this world,
But in the next,
That they weren't complicit in murder.

Sand, sand
On the potter's wheel of the sun,
On the ephemeral tremble of a shadow,
On fast-moving saigas[25],
Sand in spinneys and on lop-eared grass,
Sand in our mouths.

9

Past the Don steppe,
Past Stavropol, across the Terek river,
To Soviet held Mozdok,
To my own people – Russia,
And Russia wants to know who I am,

Collaborator, spy, coward?
New life brings new fear.

We're transported
To the Headquarters of The North Caucasus' Military District,
The commission's housed in the railway school
On the outskirts of the republic's capital.
Zadnepruk and I will be questioned together
Larichev, with his good looks, youth and receding hairline,
(he'll grow a paunch early – if he survives)
Tries to charm his way in with us,
But we walk off without him.
Zadnepruk and I go down Mozdok's crooked streets,
Past the roaring Terek,
Did it sound the same in Lermontov's days,
Or those of the Scythians, the Alans?
The river echoes the noise of our times,
Of our hearts,
Everything astounds us,
Our senses are heightened to posters,
An actor from Moscow's in town,
A lecture on the Regional Committee's new report
"Grünwald and Slavic Unity",
To buses – full of passengers,
To a fat bulb-eyed shoeshine woman,
To the felt-hatted soldiers, neat in cavalry twill,
To a lanky old Ossetian who reads at a newsstand
With his head thrown back. To cellars
Where's there's lots of wine to drink,
If you can pay –

Shall we drink for courage,
I say to Zadnepruk,
Not so much because I want to,
But because it's good to feel power

Return with money.
After the hard, terrible journey,
The encirclement,
The nights on the primitive steppe,
Not now, says Zadnepruk,
His sharp eyes squint,
As he hugs me, like a brother and says,
I'll lose my mind if I drink
And then open up my soul
He gestures wide, and says,
We must have our wits about us right now,
We need to be smart –

And then we arrive
At a wide railway track, forgotten under the dust.
I think I see Sergeant Larichev ahead,
And say to Zadnepruk, *That bastard,*
He's found the school's address
Gone there first, denounced us –
Zadnepruk says, *It's not him,*
He wants to live.
Zadnepruk's reflective when he speaks,
I know exactly what he means to say,
We stare at each other,
My encirclement brother and I,
His gaze is clear, steady.
Ten minutes later we round a bend
And see reed covered houses,
Which makes me feel at home,
The school's large burnt out yard
Still smokes in parts –
Grass grows between its sharp stones,
And officers, my fellows,
Sit around,
Commanders who've lost their armies,

Commanders with no corps, no divisions,
Wait to be checked.

Some scare each other with,
Remember what happened to Vasya Petunin,
Vasily Karpovich, Lieutenant-General?
He's a Captain now – in a penal colony!
Others, the quiet ones,
Have small bottles of vodka,
Salt in rags, tomatoes, bread,
Homemade soldier's knives,
There with them on the ground.
A man in blue trousers with general's stripes
In a worn but brightly embroidered Hutsul[26] shirt,
Talks sluggishly to a sailor, a Commander,
Who for some reason wears a laurel sellers' cap,
There are wounded men here and there too.
It's August, the Caucasus' sun
Burnishes my Don Steppe tan again.

A man in an impressive Tank General's uniform,
Says to Zadnepruk, *Et tu Brute?*
They were saying you're in prison!
Turns out you were on the run all this time!
He looks thinner than the person whose uniform he wears,
Whose medals he's got hold of
And lined up in two rows across his chest
He gives Zadnepruk a warm kiss,
They'd probably served together in the First Cavalry.
A pleased Zadnepruk introduces me to the General
Who simply shakes my hand, man to man,
And tells me his soon-to-be-famous name.
The First Lieutenant comes out of the school
With a list; everyone's quiet.
He's of average height, this thin, Caucasian Lieutenant,

He still doesn't know what war is,
Wears an unbelievably white uniform,
His high boots of kid leather,
Shine like an eastern fairy-tale.
He purses his thimble-small, juice-berry lips,
Before he utters a word,
Holds them open for a moment.
Everyone's soul dies in that hiatus,
Guard Engineer Colonel Didyk,
Prepare Major General Zhornikov!
He speaks exactly like our Leader,
When he gave the speech,
I am addressing you,
Brothers and sisters …
And so, without his cap, in soldiers' putties,
Hopeless Didyk mounts the wooden steps,
He's cut himself shaving too quickly,
The First Lieutenant looks at this tall man
With compassionate disdain,
While somewhere in the yard,
Zhornikov prepares to account for his division,
Lost like a needle in the haystack of the Sal'sk steppe.
Then it'll be Zadnepruk's turn, then mine.

But I don't know anything about it yet,
I'm still in Krasnodar, where it's spring,
The first spring of the war,
I've arrived leading the drivers with their lorries,
I've got orders to report to the rear
Of the Southern Front's Headquarters.
I've got rooms in Pomazan's family's clay-walled hut,
I'm no fool who lives in barracks,
I've just jumped off a tram,
I stand still, unsure where to go,
An inert Lieutenant-Quartermaster,

That time takes, like a river,
Inert, I float, float, float

1961–1963

ENDNOTES

1   A Soviet Quartermaster was in charge of stores, in the Imperial Army his equivalent, the Technical- Quartermaster, was responsible for intelligence.

2   Kollektivnoye Khozyaistvo – collectively owned farm.

3   A special kind of sabre; a very sharp, single-edged, single-handed, and guardless sword.

4   A Russian military shirt-tunic comprising a pullover style garment with a standing collar having double button closure.

5   State owned farm – implication of neo-serfdom.

6   Poalei Zion – a Zionist Socialist organization.

7   A reference to Perek Shira (The Song of The Universe) variously attributed to Kings David or Solomon, or to the Mishnaic sages Rabbis Akiva, Nechunia ben Hakanah and Eliezer ben Hurkenos.

8   Messieur(s).

9   An ironic hint at Stalin's speech July 3, 1941, 11 days after the German invasion, an unusually warm and unofficial appeal to the Soviet people to fight against the enemy.

10   Established January 24, 1938.

11   An ironic hint at Lenin's slogan "Party is intellect, the honour and conscience of our epoch."

12   Oka Ivanovich Gorodovikov (1879 – 1960) was a Soviet cavalry general of Kalmyk ethnicity, a Hero of the Soviet Union.

13   Commonly known as a Luger (pistol).

14   Pompotekh (pomoshnik po tekhnicheskoy chasty) – Chief of Ordnance.

15   Alludes to Stalin's address at the Kremlin Palace to the graduates of the Red Army's Academy on May 4, 1935 "In the period of reconstruction the staff, and the cadres decide everything."

16   A nomad Ulus's tent.

17   In wartime letters were folded triangle fashion, there were no envelopes.

18   The USSR received a huge amount of food aid from her allies during WW2.

19   Printing machine for small printing jobs.

20   Special battalions who stood behind the front line and shot retreating infantry pursuant to Stalin's infamous decree, called, "Not a single step back." Signed on July 28 1942.

21   Divnoye (Дивное) – marvellous (Russ.).

22   Priyutnoe (Приютное) – cosy (Russ.).

23   Izobilnoye (Изобильное) – plentiful (Russ.).

24   Styopa – diminutive of Stepan/Stephen.

25   The steppe antelope.

26   An ethno-cultural group of Ukrainian highlanders who have inhabited the Carpathian mountains, mainly in the Ukraine and northern extremities of Romania, for centuries.

The Cooperative of Deaf-Mutes

Sea makes a horizon that encrusts
The hot city street with live salt,
A tram rings past a workshop,
A deaf cooperative.
He leans over a shirt,
She, tired of sewing,
Runs a void along a line
Stitched by her machine.
This mute cooperative
Doesn't hear anything
Except what's outside
The mosquito nets at their windows,
Southern hops, the world's midday
Breath, are we lost
You, my poor verse, and I?
Have we joined a mute cooperative?

1960

In No Faith, Freedom, Love

Speak about the cost of war
The sweet illusion that life's not begun,
Of how you are yet to be born.

Who can say what day will bring?
Will birds speak? Will lightening cleave shadows
In thunderstorms, and make you welcome explosions?

Would you trust yourself,
Would you ask why you're laughing?

1940

Ghosts

We'll magnify our leaders' portraits,
Make solemn declarations,
Churn out landscapes as decreed.
Hacks, amateurs,
The untalented,
I'm one of you, I'm yours.

We, who knew what was wrong ourselves
Condemned to the shame
Of our miserable fate.
With savings in the bank,
We're still the unreliable boys
God wanted us to be.

Unreviewed in print,
We're ghosts
No one knows about.
Unbroken though bent,
Barely awake to God
We write.

About those who gasp,
Weighted-down
With tears and shame,
Stuck in the mud
Of self-reproach,
But who persist.

And tell Russia
That only we are the living
And the Temple subsists,
That only we descend
From Jeremiah
For our sins.   75

1957

Early Summer

We lost the Battalion's seal
While loading up to get out of Jolly's farm,
We've already been replaced there
And the Command's not Russian.

As Remington semi-automatics rattled
We set up a table under a cherry tree,
The Battalion Commander grinned,
God bailed us out today,

And Nikita Ivanovich, our (Party) instructor,
Knitted his blond brow
At the Manych river, which shone like a blade
Still warm with blood.

Can he, abandoned by faith
Understand what's worse, the sea's loss,
Or the roar of the red-grey water,
Or the echo of German curses?

So much that's bitter has risen overnight,
What can the dawn promise him?
The militant sparkle of the river,
Early summer flowers?

Sarcasm twists his lips
His clear mind shines in his eyes
His features aren't crude
Fear has refined them.

Oh instructor Nikita Romashenko
If only you'd survived to see
The suffocation, fear and pain
I feel in early summer's sweet air.

Deaf to German cannon,
Foreign language,
But threatened again by people
Who reject the rule of law.

I wait stupefied for the fated end,
Only one thought haunts me,
That I must bury my fear deep
And my smile is ugly.

1949

I Bought You My Thoughts

I bought you my thoughts,
The tremble of my dreams,
Children of reason, madness,
Cousins of pigeons and serpents.
I bought you my insurrection,
Smouldered quietly.
Terrified of prison[1],
I radiated heat,
Burned in darkness,
Reigned cringing at the feast,
Brought you my litanies,
Sing them when I die.

1982

My Friend[2]

When her husband and son
Were lead to the kingdom of the deaf,
Human grief changed
To an animal's roar,

Night-searched, dry-eyed
She neither grieved nor convulsed
At Lubyanka's small window
Near its House of Meetings,

The clever talked to her freely,
But she heard only the grave,
Distant,
Only the grave.

They bought charms, gifts,
Finery,
To you Khokhlushka, Tatarka,
Katspaka,

Who heard only the grave.
All this happened,
Happened,
And never swam away.

1960

This and That

Rousseau told us his beautiful dream
About how the world found peace
And men became innocent.

They worked the land,
Lived by honest work,
Ploughed, herded, piped,

Sang from the heart
While boys played with
Hoops and sticks.

Jean-Jacques did you ever dream
About the settlements near Kurgan-Tuba
Where Mujiks[3] deported from Samara
Live behind barbed wire
In wild encampments
Where no blade of grass leaf grows?

Where desert extends anguish,
Tigers trumpet in the distance,
Cotton grows from sand
Children wither on CheKa's land.

I stopped there once,
Drank with the commandant,
Soso[4] threatened me from a portrait,
And I thought about singing from the heart.

1960

Funeral

Emaciated by her eighteen year term,
Our tiny, myopic Tatyana Vasilievna's died.
Shapovalov and Horowitz from the gulag
Say a simple goodbye, no prayers, no ritual;
Why search for the betrayer as the coffin slides
Into the City's crematorium?

The exhausted tundra, whitened by insults,
Beaten by hard labour, sobs, bleeds from old wounds,
Cries out from Russia's heart –
Dissident.

Why are we sinners so keen
To ruminate over destiny
While our tiny surrogate meets it –
Why do we call her a saint
Instead of remembering her
Like pagans with Slavic rites?

Her friends are going now
To be swallowed up in Moscow's spaces,
Only Shapovalov and Horowitz
Remain in the airless City.

1958

The Taiga

Zakamye's[5], empty cathedrals,
High fences, snarling snitches, wood cabins
As harsh as predators, jailors, fraudsters,
Households where moss stuffs the narrow grooves
Between logs, cafés where breath is the wild wind
Which carries a smell of thieves and jackals.
This is the exiled Kulaks' ark
Heavy with the smell of camp stew,
Where each man seems to be fettered
With rivets of death.[6]
There is something dreadful in your constant chatter
Something good in your unkempt tangles
Chaldon[7], drunkard, wit, I come to recognise
The sick, shining look in your eyes when you grin,
The five-fingered flame of your forest fires
As we drive on a gazik[8] through your bestial,
Vile, mushroom Taiga swamp,
Where terror emerges from beauty,
Foal bells ring sadly
And strange unnamed graves
Lie under well-made crosses.
Where the steppe opens suddenly
Like it does in the Caucasus
But here there's no freedom in their story,
Only four sides, four norths,
Four zones, four abysses
Where laws rot in the four walls
Of penal servitude,
Where day seems to me to drag on
Like a black marketeer
Or safecracker
Wearing the tatters of a jacket
On the day he's freed from a convoy.

The sky threatens, as motionless as the convoy's eyes,
With the rigid blue of Russia's hungry villages.
Have you ever been in a cordoned off place
Where the pine's as timid as a doe?
Where friendship[9] makes fathers, vagabonds, murderers alike
Into lumberjacks and brings them to the taiga
To kill. How long is it since felling's plague
Raged in the forest, since axe blows
Seemed wiser than sacred knowledge,
Trees fell like Jews, and every ditch became a Babi Yar?
Have you seen the hangman's leavings?
The larch's joyful body cut down,
Forced to the ground? Have you seen
The pride with which a fir dies?
Tell me, did you stay silent
As they did, or stoop to curse the murderers?
Did you tread water
While the rights of plants were abused?
Why do we make war against the forest's tribes,
For books, watch towers, do gas ovens
Need firewood? Why do we execute trees
Which take revenge at our insane power,
Which break us into two parts,
Where thief guards thief?
When will you, the taiga,
The green director of public prosecution,
Acquit us of our crime,
Address us, a miserable community
Of suffering?

1962

Drawing of a Greek Square

The verandah and the terrace
Are both spooled with grey ivy.
Should I leave here quickly,
What do I have to say?
This city hasn't changed its clothes,
I'm not an upstart any more,
Even if Madam Theophal still blushes.
The square's still crowded, napping drivers
Have parked their taxis in the shade,
So it's easy to get to Kherson, Izmail, Reni …
Why do I, the loser, get angry,
Do I already want to forget Vasilia
Who sneaked into the shed thirty years ago
Bolted the door behind her
As though winding a mechanical toy,
Thrilled with her shameless laugh,
Burned my lips with fever which never quenched,
Vacationing undergraduate
Wasn't it yesterday
Your feeble soul warbled about death,
The good who were executed,
Timid insurgent who saw
Dark whirlpools
In the eyes of the mad peasants
Who lay side by side
On the platform at Zhmerinka
Unable to stand up or leave,
Scheduled by old ordinances.
Ruled to be kurkuls[10] then, branded
Who saw the wild Ukrainian sky,
The gold reserves of the stars,
The wild cost of bread
The pain of crazed eyes fade

In the spark of these black southern nights
Before that easy, fast, mad, love of yours,
With cheerful dark nudity
Ready to swell with heavy Greek beauty
Ready to collapse?
85

1960

The Executioner

The first sergeant earns
A hundred and fifty rubles a month,
At forty he's the same age
As his buxom wife.

Their daughter's good at violin
Which she studies at music school,
While he spends his nights
Working as a sort of sniper.

He never sees the faces
Only signs, only the signs
Sorrow draws with such diligence
In the suburban darkness.

He follows orders, fires at the chest,
Or forehead – unperturbed which,
His boss likes to give him a wink,
"Just what the doctor ordered!"

Twenty years ago he beat the Germans,
Now he dispatches the condemned –
Contraband clothes, wine,
Traded by the Georgian or Bryansker –

He wakes up at midday. Drinks cognac.
Has mouth polyps from smoking on an empty stomach –
He's stopped. His throat is hoarse.

His wife knows nothing,
It's the happiest of marriages,
She doesn't know he'll soon die of cancer.

1965

Nestor and Saria

A story from the Caucasus

1

I've heard that animals can
Show selfless devotion,
Fight against evil, exchange glances
In which we recognise the human.
Will I ever forget you, Naya,
My light bay Kalmyk filly?
The storm of war made us friends.
Will I forget your brilliant eyes,
The dark terror of that barn
Where we both hid from the Germans
And each sighed about our own?

2

But man's different, accept this,
Whether you're friend or enemy.
Perdition, achievement, spirit,
Flesh, blood; separated in animals,
Are folded into man, fused,
Like radioactivities made to relate,
In a way which scares non-humans
But which would choose death to be born,
And are called Reason, Love.

3

Many tales have been created about this,
One of them lives in my heart.
I met the Abkhazians at the Black Sea,
A particle of humanity, a nation.
While Egypt erected pyramids

Of stone, grief, resentment,
The Abkhazians made wine in presses,
Accumulated warm fleeces,
Shot wild nanny goats in the woods of Colchis
And sang at will, with no worries;
According to honest Herodotus' account.

4

There were those taught by the Greeks
To pray to the crucified who'd cross themselves,
While muezzins shouted at others
Calling for the righteous struggle,
But the pagan heroes are still heard
In the mountains and surf.
There are new stories.
And I'll tell you one
Which I'm sure affects the earth,
My fate, yours, the NKVD-GB's.

5

What inspired the myth maker?
Days when eyes watched valleys
Which never changed, the person
Who saw ships as distant, foreign;
1920 when Nestor, prominent Bolshevik,
Hid in a Muslim family's peasant hut,
Told his host about his exploits,
Shared news of a country which thundered
Far away from Abkhazia

6

Slim and wiry as a greyhound
He sat night after night
At his shelter's narrow entrance

Watching the Earth's amazing clothes,
Silver Birch's close friend the Cypress,
Grape vines which clung to Mountain Ash,
The nobility manifest as trees united
Grasses cooperated, peaks marbled,
Valleys burnt rose; where there were branches
Laden with figs and pomegranates,
The Slav apple's Transcaucasian brother.

7

It may be in nature's accord's an illusion
That it harbours hostility, that trees fight
Like people, that in their war
Life begins. Nestor wasn't drawn
To such heights. He thought,
The Mensheviks are in Tiflis,
Waiting around languidly is purposeless,
But it isn't time to make a move yet
I must react like a fox not a tiger,
The family I'm with are nice
And Saria's as good as happiness.

8

But what's happiness?
A statement of tempting, borrowed phrases?
The liberation of indigenous people?
Being part of the explosion
Which shook the whole world?
A ravishing, calculated battle,
A fortune hunter's cunning trap,
Power over people which is so great
That they're too scared to curse you
Because you're as unshakable as prayer?
Or the shine of God in the give of brown eyes?
At that troubled time Nestor didn't know.

9

The girl in her sixteenth spring
Didn't ask questions
When she, covering her face with her hand,
Greeted him shyly.
Happiness
Was the prematurely aged Nestor,
Unshaven, not tall,
Who reasoned strangely with her father,
And brother, who put a stop to harassment
Both by the infidels' deity, and the Koran,
To whom fate was clear,
And who gave her a share in it.

10

Protecting the new laws of life, Nestor listened,
Was attentive to her father
Who's talk about rising prices,
Seemed endless to her.
Then explained Moscow's decrees,
Warmed their meaning, with Lenin's breath,
Spoke for her
But without looking at her,
Who gave advice on farming,
Touched their anxious hearts,
Like a winemaker's aphartsa[11].

11

Nestor said goodbye to them
Like a man who cares for tradition
Drank well from a cold pitcher,
A horn of homemade wine,
Thanked them with respect,
Was calm, dignified not terse.

Jumped onto his saddle, in cowl and burka,
Disturbed the reeds when he spurred his horse.
Did he look lovingly once at least?
Saria didn't come out on the threshold
When her new road began.

12

Did anything that happened on Earth
Care about her dreams?
The British left for home,
The red flag was raised in Sukhum-Kale,
And although the press is inspired, its colours grey,
One vivid newspaper arrived which showed Nestor,
Military jacketed, medal breasted, podiumed
Like an Abkhazian leader.
The page was on the table in front of everyone,
But she saw him tearing away on his horse.

13

It was a warm, damp morning.
A boat from Batumi was moored
At Sukhumi pier. There was a bee
Looking for special honey, which buzzed in a hive
As if she didn't see the Greeks in fezzes,
The dandies in leggings and Circassian coats,
The farmers coming down slowly from mountains,
The Armenians travelling in chaises,
Or the languid sadness of Odesa's brokers, craft,
And tradespeople who'd heard,
The Red Army had arrived.

14

Southerners are judgmental
And everything here breathed with the South.
But what did sea-shore coffee house gossip
Sound like, look at? She was invisible to it.
A peasant girl in flat shoes and a black shawl
Carrying a pre-war carton box to go to the Riviera Hotel,
A terrible journey to set out on,
Everyone knew it was Revkom's[12] headquarters.

15

The story goes, should it be believed,
That Nestor saw Saria through the window.
But may not have gone to her at first,
When he knew she was there,
But he read the truth in her eyes,
Light, free as space,
Stronger than her brother's anger,
Her Father's threats,
Her mother's bitter tears,
The fortress stronghold of Islam …
Then he understood, credited her,
Said to Revkom, "This is my wife."

16

In learning to speak Russian or draw an image[13]
She saw signs of the progress to come,
Of education abroad, the Spring of statehood.
Those were the days when everything was new,
Created for the first time; factories, hospitals,
Tractors, text books, army anthems, CheKa,
The dead and living stock of fate.
How often the work of past innocence
Suddenly rampages like an axe.

17

The luxury of uniform and military stars
Of holidays resplendent when no one shot
At anyone but only into the air,
When Nestor's son Rauf was born
When they both took their places of influence
Accepted fealty, feasted, joked, drank long and hard,
Did well by their mistress,
Who'd been a loyal and loving wife,
Who came to her husband with her head ducked,
Who hadn't idled as she might've done.

18

Their house was like an iced cake,
A tower surrounded by a steep semicircle,
Which faced the subtropical Riviera,
It sat on a gentle slope of blue asphalt
Lush with flower gardens
Like the medieval pictures of heaven,
With waterfalls, laid out from drawings
Made by Saria, the region's beautiful first lady,
Who everyone knew was a friend
Of crafty Lavrentiy's wife.

19

Two names rang out under Stalin,
Those of Lavrentiy and Sergo, Sergo a soldier,
People's Commissar, the kartvel's[14] comrade,
Who knew Lenin. Lavrentiy had no past,
Could wear a Circassian or a tailcoat,
Because his world never changes,
He thought, *no,* and smiled, *yes.*
The leader immediately saw an oprichnik[15]
In this limited intellect, a field
In which he could shine.

20

The Father of the people, his wise light,
Often rested in a seaside villa
Which Nestor prepared for him
With love and kindness,
Stalin rested, enjoyed the hospitality
Of the multilingual Eastern land
Where even the hierarchy of mountain peaks
Was an iron consequence of reason
And a half wild member of the CIK[16]
Seemed to please the lord
More than all the crowing leaders of the day.

21

Back in Moscow, the past's offspring still existed
Its threaded trunk hadn't been crushed
Trotsky lurked through his pince-nez
And the undestroyed names were legion;
Zinoviev[17], well-educated but inept;
Kamenev[18], an arrogant Jewish nobleman;
Radek[19], a tiresome fidget;
Tomsky[20], jumped up,
And the hateful scholar Bukharin[21]
One of a kind with his clever brilliance,
A world class tribal leader.

22

Under the shade of the eucalyptus
In the bay, was this where he, the slow, patient,
Good gardener, nursed the terrible fruit?
Was it here he realised
In the calm of South's autumn,
"We can achieve nothing
Until the trouble makers

Are turned to dust,
Removed, cut down, layer by layer."
Wasn't it here he yearned for the arrival,
Of the century's thirty-seventh brutal year?

23

And Russia began to move; sceptics,
Brigade commanders, scatterbrains,
Moujiks[22], peasants, Putilov plant workers
Poles, Noblemen, old Bolsheviks, engineers,
Creeping empiricists, CheKa officers,
Dissenters, mullahs, Esperantists,
Double-dealers, dashnaks, sailors,
Mistresses, the talented, the fools,
Predel'schiks[23], lishentses[24], vitalists,
Neighbours, Leningraders, the old,
Students, relatives, jokers.

24

Alash Hordes[25], whiners
Basically every miserable victim who'd survived
The peck of life's unyielding rooster on his back,
Was sent to the edge of the Polar night,
Where rare flashes of light, which barely were blotted out,
By the lonely, scurvied Taiga[26].
Where there was no one
To commemorate with obelisks,
Where men burned without gas,
Where shooting followed shooting,
Where loved ones turned away from one another,
Where venom oozed drop by drop while rumour dribbled,
Spirit stenched, rotted, exhausted itself.

25

Lavrentiy smiled and asked Nestor,
What's your real name?
I've heard, don't laugh at the rumour,
That you chose your nickname
To honour Makhno[27].
I was baptized, Nestor.
Don't be angry,
Lavrentiy embraced the Abkhaz leader,
But Nestor understood the message,
The purpose of Lavrentiy's visit,
Their feud seethed true,
Aged like wine.

26

We are sinners, young and old.
And yet the world's erected on a saint.
Where is the righteous? Just start to look for him,
He's among us and in us, we are growing with him.
He's often selfish, like us, hateful to himself,
Vain, treacherous, cowardly, miserable, cruel,
Lustful, he longs for false instead of bitter truth.
And what, you ask, is his holiness? Only in one thing,
The ideal, that isn't extinguished in him.

27

The ideal, it happens, is negligible,
The righteous itself is funny, small,
But would you be able to pull its sword
Out of its sheath?
Go to your death for an ideal?
And in many respects Nestor was a sinner
He humbled himself before the Gori god[28],
Knew the price of a trick,

Could walk above truth,
On curved roads.
When did he harden into a crystal?
When he represented Abkhazia.

28

He loved everything about his nation,
Its customs, epics, princes,
Whom he never challenged.
Turned it into a kind of living museum.
Destroyed, under official pressure,
Only one in a hundred Kulaks,
Was firmly committed
To Abkhazia and sought friends for her
In Moscow's People's Commissariats.

29

Wanting to understand Stalin,
You could be surprised by his wish,
To make the Caucasus a bastion
Of his power in the East.
Paris was said to be worth a Mass,
The Abkhazians' and Circassians' value eluded him,
Nestor's motives were questioned,
Lavrentiy's too, Nestor's self interest,
Evidenced by his reliance on his assistant Sergo[29]

30

And Sergo hated Lavrentiy
Raged that he was a "Musavatist thief",
A toady with someone else's biography,
Asked how the leader had failed to expose
The lecherous, killer of the Caucasus,
Who became a source of stinking mud,

Unknown betrayals and crimes,
Who'd soon destroy, "our framework"-
Sergo raged inside, while Nestor,
Surrounded by Abkhazia's mountains,
Conversed, quietly, confidentially,
With the People's Commissar.

31

In Moscow, the regular Plenary Session over,
Sergo led the Abkhazian to Stalin.
Who met them in his usual military jacket,
Didn't shake hands, said to Sergo,
Eagle, you're fatter!
Didn't look at Nestor
The shelves held odd volumes of Plekhanov[30],
Pushkin was pinned to the wall with thumb tacks
There were bottles and glasses on a white-clothed table,
Which stood on a washed, village-style floor,

32

And guards breathed somewhere behind the walls,
But the leader's halo didn't tarnish,
He looked alert, fiery, drunk,
Gestured carelessly, *You've come,*
So drink Dvin[31], *it's expensive.*
Then Nestor said of Lavrentiy, *He's a traitor,*
Gives himself airs,
Undermines the Leader in the Republic,
The leader sipped, *Kinto*[32], *swindler,*
He promoted himself to Marxists!
The laughter was warm, the look weighty.

33

Nestor went home elated,
His hopes finally realised.
He waited and waited for the call.
He was summoned to the bureau in Tbilisi,
Lavrentiy had invited him to dinner.
The driver brought in a couple of dozen bottles of Kachich.[33]
Nestor got back to his room after three p.m.
When did he let out his final breath?
His body was found in his bed.
A massive heart attack.
The most senior doctors concurred.

34

His body was sent to Abkhazia
With due respect, where Saria said
*I know you were poisoned by Lavrentiy
Nestor, my life, my soul*!
The Republic's papers carried long obituaries
And Nestor's portrait, but after a year
His corpse was taken from his grave at night,
It was said, *The people decided.*
It didn't stop there, Saria was taken,
Here starts the track of her next incarnation.

35

The Kremlin didn't sleep that dawn.
Suddenly the drivers' yawning was interrupted,
A shot rang out an office somewhere,
Narkom had been killed, by whom?
Suicide? Damn the guards.
The leader appeared, in his Moroccan boots,
Trod softly, as menacingly as fate,
Moved his lower lip a little,

His friend lay dead.
Stalin looked at Sergo for a minute,
Then cursed *Hana!*[34] in his [Georgian] slang.

   36

And in Abkhazia, the sea, sun
Holiday houses, alcohol, myrtle,
Flirting were joined by grief,
There was a prison cell for Saria, thirty-three,
Her son was fourteen. She'd known work
On the land, on dry clay,
A poor house woven from branches,
Receptions at the Kremlin,
The glitter of fairies on capitols,
The sound of feasts, soft feather beds,
Then prison, wouldn't she go crazy?
Didn't she know winter was coming?

   37

The trial began. Shocked Abkhazians
Came to know that in the silence
Nestor wove intrigue, he spied,
Lived in Kemal Pasha,
Wanted to give Abkhazia to the Turks,
No wonder he loved
Hoods and burkas, feudal antiquity.
Taught his relatives his passion,
To his colleagues, he was greedy, selfish,
Curt, unmasked now, how foul
A traitor without honour and soul.

   38

Lavrentiy, director of the spree,
Believed every player mattered,

There were no bit parts, the wife's evidence
Would crown the trial, the school
Of his direction is the relevant and correctly reconstructed
Landscape called psychological realism.
She was threatened, beaten,
Kept on the block, given full-bodied blows
In a way that upset even
Our formidable high officials.

   39

Now, tell me, tell me now, you whore,
Now, tell me bitch. Six nights interrogation.
The chief above her, near her ear,
Rattled the keys like a treasurer.
She persisted, *He was a crystal,*
Who raised Abkhazia out of the ruins,
He was a good husband and father,
Stalin's iron, solid fighter,
When he finds out he'll punish you,
Lavrentiy and your other hangmen!
And there were six keys in the bunch.

   40

They brought her brother. He was mad, sick
Sister, confess, Nestor's guilt.
I wish my older brother were pleased with me,
But I don't remember, are you my brother?
They brought her son. He was a living wound,
Look, they've knocked all my teeth out,
Nana,[35] *confess and they'll let us go home!*
You are my life, Rauf, my son,
But is a life created for deception?
And teeth, what are they for?
You know, children often have toothache.

41

Pulled out her hair, strand by strand,
Look, the long braids are gone.
Well, what's this? Does she break?
Keeps silent, vile thing. Continue.
Frightening, owl-like, nods,
Her bloody, bald head at random,
But what a strong and wonderful look,
What live faith burns there,
Question, blow, question, blow, question...
I scream, but you won't see my tears.

42

Her brown eyes are stuck with pins
And there is no more intelligence
As they invert, she doesn't break then either.
Then locks and bolts aren't needed any more, she's dead.
Why were the mountain's silent?
Caucasia, you wear a shroud,
Why do you hide the story from the world?

43

The war's winter. Moscow besieged.
Letters emerged from the Lefortovo[36] basement,
Said, "Dear Uncle Lavrentiy," cried Rauf's tears,
Had Lavrentiy forgotten him? No,
Rauf was brought out and shot.
Before he died he dreamed of his mother,
My son, you didn't have to write to him.
Believe me, it's better to die in a basement.
And there, in the snow, our soldiers fought,
And began a new crossing.

44

We still were prepared to wait
For many years, to remember those
Who carried a heavy cross,
But the widows return from exile
Who left at the age of brides.
The country attends loud readings.
We learn that truth lived
In the dark, in jails, ashes sepulchral urns,
Grew up among the living,
And now we hear it in capacious words,
Imprisoned for a quarter of a century,
Set free by the twentieth congress[37].

45

The Abkhaz spring, breezes with freedom,
The Euxine Pontus[38] hisses the alarm.
The luminary's statue is removed,
Nestor replaces it at the garden's entrance,
In front of the monument, an elder sits on the bench,
Cloaked over his beaver lamb vest,
He's hook-nosed, round-shouldered, dry, yellow,
Once he asked questions, now he's penniless of course,
But he hasn't changed, still looks the same

46

As when he stuck pins in Saria's eyes,
He's retired now. His wife's dead,
His daughter's in the glavk[39],
His nickname for her's "girlie"
He drinks coffee in "Amre[40],"
Reads books about Byzantium, the Mongol yoke,
Plays backgammon. How can he be understood?
He looks so human,

But if you know the history,
You don't need to force an open door,
Only say to people, *He's an animal.*

    47

And a focused, polite, self-assured
Eighth-grade child nods at him.
Spring roars ahead
Like school holidays
Welcomed by fathers and mothers.
Dawn becomes clearer,
The sea bluer and bluer,
Sings about the Argonauts
Who sailed for truth amid raging lies,
Sings about their native Prometheus,
And the future which runs
In the swell of their sea
Look, it's waving its hand to us.

1962

Evening in Lykhny[41]

I remember the tender bell
Of Abkhazia's compline[42]
And the eucalyptus' sleep
Overhung by leaves
That caress in the air,
The smell of grapes
And the golden fingernail
Of the young moon.
I remember the warble
Of the Nightingale
In early spring
As April clamped a flute
Between its lips.
I remember a meeting
With the slender-waisted,
Gray elders,
As the Dioskurian verse
Chimed then trailed off.

1991

Solikamsk in August 1962

I don't believe maternity homes
And learned books have engendered eras

As numerous as the wisdom
Sunk in the forests of the Perm Great[43] and Small[44],

Where deep in the past
New civilizations began to rule

I don't believe there's a second covenant,
Not even between man and his axe,

That has caused shrines to crumble.
Sorrow doesn't leave salt in a cooling tower

For years this place,
Where conifers were sovereign,

Rhymed tears with fear, roamed sadness
With torn nostrils[45], blushed all the garnets[46],

Of salt mined at Stroganov with convicts' blood
But the idol gods didn't help Voguls,

Ostyaks and fugitive convicts and fetishes bowed
To Russia's hard currency.

In the wooden seventeenth century three-stoned churches
Assembled, resplendent, on the square

Where snow was replaced by dust and dirt.
A bloated, old, gray merchant's house sat

Behind the churches. Now it's an hotel for officers
Who live everywhere and protect us,

Because we need to be watched.
Whether I come down from the mountains,

Or through seaside back gardens,
Push onto a bus, visit little coy parks,

The "Forester" restaurant, or the "Metallurgist" cinema,
Filled with soldiers, matinees and evenings,

It seems to me I'm in a game, watched
In the green twilight, by hounds and hunters

Who haven't yet decided whether to kill,
Cook and eat me or invite me

To sit at their sides –
At a distance, on a hill, there are new suburbs,
Modern, well appointed houses, I climb up to them,
Tire, and from the summit see the camp,

Its watch towers, lit for some reason,
In the daytime. Amid the city, schools,

Food stores, pharmacies, workshops,
Reading rooms and district committees,

There's a camp and the taiga, there are log roads
And the convoys –

What are centuries of human experience,
Revolutions, insights, discoveries?

In one moment, one turn of events
The law of learned books flies to hell,

Gives way to the laws of the taiga,
The canons of wood cutters, gospels of wolves,

Inquisitions of jackals. I visit the city
Knowing the fugitives' search company's sergeant

And corporal are behind me.
I spot them, remember their signs,
They prowl waddle, dress in mufti[47],
But our courageous gavriks[48], we the people know better,
From your khaki shirts which give you away.

I think, about keeping a secret
From the omniscient, scoundrel oper[49],

Saving my bread ration for a whole month,
Or making a silent escape to the fence

Where the earth's been dug up,
While Lezghin, the convoy guard
Stands up to have sex with a teenage schoolgirl.

Running into the forest's darkness,
Confusing the dogs,

Drawing close to swampy perdition, midges' sly wails,
To be betrayed by leaf[50] and branch.
Learning animal fear and starvation,
Straying in wading mosses, on ridge, in hollow,

Stealing lichen and tinder from poor squirrels
And finally getting to the city on that August night,

Hiding in a cattle-wagon, dreaming of a house,
A peasant woman at the station called "Nowhere",

Or a railway siding called "Toad",
Klaxons, footsteps, whistles, night arrests, lights,

And the fugitives' search company have got you
Safe in iron bracelets and anklets

You fall quietly on your stomach on a dirty cell floor
A table, feet up, is turned over on your back –

Now, believe me, they'll take your soul out of you.
A soldier will jump across the table,

He'll work by the sweat of his brow,
Beat away your liver and your lungs,
Leave no scratches on your body,
You're sick, dying – in two weeks

You'll be free of this, you know brother,
A wood jacket won't warm you in the earth.

The sergeant and corporal head to the station
And we go there too. The first thing we'll see

Is wasteland and a red light district
Full of slander and its apprentices,
The usual suspects, taunters,
Call it the Eighth of March[51] quarter.

In the distance there's an unnamed camp
With a narrow entrance –
Two people can't get in at once,
Immediately to the left there's a police door,

To the right, the opera house, tribunal, reprisals
A gloomy hallway leads to a wide assembly room,

Worthy of a witness's description,
Two families sit on benches there,

Ukrainians from Transcarpathia,
Who learned a long time ago

That we're blood brothers.
Their children were born in the taiga,

But there is an order –
"Let them go home at the happy hour."

The gathering's really international,
Udmurts, Volga Germans, a Cossack,

Jehovah's Witness –
Who'd served long stretches,

A soldier who'd shot an escaped prisoner
And was sent on holiday to Lake Baikal[52]

At a small window, on the back wall,
Like the light of the world

Looms the obscure face of the omnipotent cashier.
The platform is silent, deserted, there are no wagons.

Look out Fedya the first sergeant –
Where's our friend been, the café?
He carries a suitcase, wears a beret, a striped waistcoat,
But trained eyes will detect an offender,

They turn on the boy who tries to break away,
They twist his hands,

Beat him in the teeth and eyes,
Science triumphs

They lead him to the opera house.
Five minutes pass, no more,

He's released – he's a fixer,
"We botched it, OK go to Berezniki."[53]

There's blood on his waistcoat, on his face, in his eyes –
Oh life, do I need you? Stop

I don't want to knock my head against a wall,
I'd rather go into the woods, howl like a wolf,
Back, back into darkness,
The cave, the Mesolithic Age,

Where the savage's spear will heal my heart.
Do you see the Mayor's ancient house?

Let's go into the museum.
There are pictures of the past around,

The Civil War. There are a few of dispatches
Which describe the region, the SR's revolt[54]
And here's the contemporary –
The plant being built,

The elected representative of the people
Who is a distinguished Perm woman,

Workers at harvest-time,
The worldwide struggle for peace and happiness,

The hard path we overcame,
But where did we get to?[55]

113

1963

Chastushka[56]

In Pachelma a village once stood,
Where crops would fail and marriages were good,
Where horses guarded at night ate grass,
Where last resting places and meadows were sparse.

In Soviet hands what grew and lived was changed,
Kulaks were de-Kulakised until they became deranged,
With stomachs which shrunk to the size of fists
They'd run away until caught for transport lists.

Switchman godfathers hid them in sidings til night,
Had this been France it'd have been worse, right?
For five thousand miles they slept like the dead
Then woke with a jolt from their moving beds,

In Tajikistan, where women wore trousers under skirts
While grass withered[57] on the Trinity, blessed.
As Mujik families got used to yurts[58]
Their rights were listed with the best.

On days off the blue-eyed, snub-nosed
Asian sprigs still crowd from near and far
And drink together on patios
To cry and sing chastushka

1961

Moonlight

City boys use probes
To look for bread from nightfall
Until the Turkish sabre moon,
Which lights up the peasant families,
Pales over the steppe shacks.
Everyone will be sent to Kotovsk[59] in an hour,
Then Kazakhstan's regions,
"Liquidated as a class."[60]
In red wagons
They'll become insomniacs,
Who'll mourn
The distortion of truth –
The grass stands proud against the wind, bows,
Stretches to the sea.
They guard persistent feebleness,
This silenced sullen people.
If a girl wants the toilet the whole convoy follows,
The door's kept open, no one runs if everyone's in sight –
I remember the steppe bathed in moonlight
And the deafness of human grief.
I met a friend in Odesa.
He's old, retired,
Hadn't escaped the common fate,
Had spent eighteen years in camp.
Did he remember dispossessing kulaks?
Probing for grain,
A breeze that unfolds grass
The moonlight which used to shine.

1963

A Hamlet

Silver brooches of clover
Whiten amiably next to the track,
Moths flutter over a lime tree.
In the river's opaque mirror
A big, foggy cloud swells
Like a pregnant woman in a sundress.

Has the devil marked this hamlet?
The cockerel's silent at dawn,
No one dreams or sobs among the limes,
The milk churns don't rattle in the barns,
There's just a long row of empty houses,
As silent as a shrouded corpse.

1983

A Nook in the Forest

This hillock's silent
By a tree trunk's hem,
The creek smells of iron
Like a person smells of warmth,

The highway's soaked
Like a towel, its dust's nailed down,
The bachelor-nightingale's about to click
In the branches.

Only some enjoy
The boundless forest,
Or understand
Its scope,

Grass, canopy,
Wild-gleamed water,
Not dark or homeless,
But lit by every star.

If I dig deep
In rot and mud
Will I find the light
Of all my Russia?

1984

Beggars in 1922

The belitsas'[61] hoods are starched,
The chernitsas'[62] faces are saddened,
Pilgrims set out to journey,
To pray without icons
To strangle without rope,
Where only pine needles lie
The Civil War's subsided,
The peasants' huts get richer,
There's lots of food, variety –
It's just a little church that's boarded up,
As though Russia were not the Lord's country,
But the home of the profaned.
The spruce needles have become verdant,
The pilgrims beg,
Receive, are repelled,
The belitsas age young,
The chernitsas die starved –
Their Sisters bury them in fields.

1987

In the Field Behind the Forest

I go into the fields with a blade of grass,
A flower's stalk?
I'm not a flower but a princess,
I wear a crown not a wreath.
I made a contribution to the monastery's coffers,
We're the retired who left the world
And were condemned to be creatures of field and forest.
We lived in cloisters with joy
Glad of the land's blessing,
But the world breathed with the plague of sickness,
Threatened, reprieved,
Marinushka[63] went one way,
Another way was paved for Annushka[64],
And where is the princess now?
I'm just a thin petal.
But I believe that we'll cure one another,
The Easter Water is close
We'll bake forty larks[65]
For forty martyrs,
And even though I became grass
We're together, together again,
We've not been sickened by the plague,
Ruined,
I call: "Is that you, Marinushka,
Are you there Annushka?"
While only aspen weeps over me,
Only earth, flowers, grass surround me.

1985

On the River Istra

It's not the stars that praise themselves,
As they glow on holy eve –
But gentle angels
Who put candles at the feet of the Mother of God.
And when starlight descends
On Palm week
It doesn't find a derelict garage,
An empty village,
But the Abbey garden which has disappeared,
Sweet apples will ripen by the bushel,
Giant loaves will be racked out for sale,
There'll be honey jars and butter pats
Near the fine-cloth factory
Thrown up in a sloboda[66].
The merry river Istra's
Seven-belled-hum is constant.
The eternal Virgin will see the nuns
Who work in the garden, who spread the canvas
She'll choose a bride for her son
Who met the world from a stable,

1986

When You Appeared to Me in My Native Town

In 1920 I thought I saw you
In the Church of the Assumption
Around the corner.
I thought you came
From a Ukrainian village
With a child conceived in hunger.
When your beauty shone
Like a golden queen
On the windows of the Chartres Cathedral
I looked into your face
And wondered if you knew
How soon your son would be crucified.
When you were at Kazan[67]
And didn't cross the Lake
Where ice and waves colluded[68]
But with your boy,
Crossed Neva's front line
To share the blockade's bread.
When you were the Sistine Madonna,
It seemed to us you had two wings
And were invisible
As you flew towards us
And kept flying
Until we lived, will live, had lived.

1987

Southern Churches

There are Uglich and Suzdal temples
Glorified whether full or empty,
Framed eternal
With a polyphony
Like the music of the grove.
There are simpler churches
In our Novorossiya[69].
They're little blue clay-walled huts,
Southern tabernacles
Set next to market-squares,
Their clothes don't shine,
Their stones glow
In the predawn mist
And gypsies play cards
In their gardens
Which grow like fishing tackle,
Vines, alive with God's word,
Caressed, pleased.
There's no tree of kings,
No antiquity, the heart buzzes
With ancient tunes,
The air of warmheartedness,
And the lyrnik's[70] lyre
Smells not myrrh
But of the Cimmerian[71] grass.

1969

Autumn at the Sea

Deserted beach, sun-lit-flare-gleamed waves,
Bright sand, tired obese fishermen
Chatty white-shirt-fronted seagulls
Black packs of thin dogs.

The fisherman's got such woman's breasts.
Where did all the mackerel and flounder go?
Odesa's elderly score goat[72],
And chat on sunbeds,

I share their fate
And knowing nothing fresher
Than the music of the interrogation in their accents,
The irony of their grammar.

A boy argued with southern poverty,
Left home fast,
Found nothing replaced the sea,
Learned nothing, nothing.

How did I get here, in whose wake,
Where did I scatter the salt of reason?
Life, what shall I do with you,
What shall I do with your simple pain?

I came back so late,
When the waves were cold,
Barely swam, came ashore,
It was thick, opaque.

1982

A May Night in the Forest

Exceptional,
The moon somehow lanterned,
Painted by Chagall,
Lit by Kabbalah's mystery,

The meadow seems to contour
Like Christ bowing a request
To a Samaritan,
With convergent birches,

How can I understand
The mark of vowels and numbers
Dim, fragrance
When an avian hero[73] exalts,

Small, almost colourless,
Unspectacular in flight,
Ingeniously inconspicuous,
He sings so well, he sings so well.

1988

Commissar

Soviet power triumphed, Kolchak[74] was defeated,
Joseph consolidated CheKa's reach in the Transbaikal[75],
Summoned the Semeiskie[76], interrogated and terrified them
With the chill in the sad velvet of his Jewish eyes,
Invaded the souls of the starover[77] women
Like a harbinger of divine wrath.
A handsome runt, this long-eyelashed Commissar,
Listened to pleas, tired, clenched his fist to his mouth,
Confused the Gubkom[78] with his holy simplicity.
By some sufferance he survived[79]
And the slope of days brought this veteran
To Siberia on Russia's fiftieth anniversary,[80]
Where his sad, velvet eyes peered
Like those of a shivering chipmunk
Searching for light in The Taiga.

1973

The Compound at Vilnius

I don't need signs or names,
I'll understand without inscriptions,
Stones say to me: "They lived here,
And no one needs to cry for them."
And it turns out they live next door
To the Episcopal church's gothic courtyard,
And even to St Peter's sacristan,
That they were close to the impoverished szlachectwo[81]
That pan[82] Jesus, in his shabby kuntush[83],
Sometimes cried for their souls.
There's no one in the medieval ghetto now
With curly hair or a Roman nose,
Only under the dimly lit arch
In the University's courtyard
Near a warehouse which stocks office furniture,
Do I come unexpectedly,
Upon my fellow countrymen,
Inert but alive, sculpted,
Mary, John, Joseph –
And the ancient courtyard
Hears us discuss trivialities.

1963

Ashes

Charred and ashen I whisper, *I've been cremated.*
In deserted barracks on Bavarian grasslands.

I think, *I'm blind, confounded*
My palate has claimed my tongue.

When Mercedes Benz' and Volkswagens
Course silently through evening autobahns

I ask *how do I find my way to Odesa*?
Born burnt, I can't yet mourn

What it means to be alive or dead.
My cold embers won't light a flame

1967

Moses

The train of my black thought
Tunnels through heaving sewers,
Races along all German, Soviet,
Polish roads and beyond.
Hurls through ovens, mortuaries,
Ravages. All manner of death.

Then for the first time
God reveals his face to me,
Intact, spiritual, lit by the blaze
Of gas inside the burning bush.

1967

Odesa's Synagogue

Its entrance is dark and dirty
Its walls dilapidated,
A cat mews from somewhere
High above the ark.
The chestnut eyed Rabbi
Wears a shabby frock coat,
He looks like a cunning child
Who could out-argue the devil
And still see the funny side.
Today's the Tora festival[84]
But this is a small congregation
With faces like tablets
Of craving and grief,
Are they genuine
Or is this also a place to be afraid
Of dull informers?
To the noise, banal conversation,
Flicker of funereal candlelight
They bring the sacred object
And their hearts beat faster.
The faded velvet[85]
Contains everything that became the beginning
And there is no end!
They cry and laugh and kiss
With resignation,
Not gold ingots
But scrolls[86] of commandment,
Essence, meaning, connection.
Dost thou see them O Lord[87]
As they circle the synagogue?[88]
I'm just a passerby,
But help me, God,
Oh, help!

1969

And[89]

Nothing's as powerful, not January's heat,
The pack's drive for freedom,
No sound, letter, word,
Nothing in the lexicon holds its mystique.

Alone it curbs the sovereign,
Differentiates, combines:
Day and night, peace and war,
Greatness and its fall,

Challenges yours and mine
Supports singularity and vision.
Names a foreign people
I've heard of

Who unite death and conception
Weekends and childhood
Freedoms and gardens
Truth, compassion,
Courage and kindness,

Space and joy,
The sad and the humane
Merge and relate,
In the small, foreign "And Tribe".

And when the expropriated idol
Joins the mother at the altar,
The world and I will be strengthened,
And I'll speak about myself.

Dictionaries are numb,
People need a gauge
Against which to antithesise
And can't live without
Its namesake nation.

131

1967

Nomads' Fire

We've lived in the empire
For over four centuries
Its interruptions breathe at us
With the birch and the nightingale
We used to be poor, threadbare,
Highway inn-keepers
Who rushed to battle fronts and barracks,
But none of that served us,
We wasted time senselessly
Both when the Nile insisted
That Leviticus used and extended
Hellenic speech and numbers,
And when poet-clothed Spanish
Rose in prayer,
As the grandee Talmud Tora
Excommunicated Spinoza from the Temple.
What is our destiny?
When will there be rest from the chase?
Or are we the nomads' fire,
Formless, eternal?
Where should we ignite again,
Take our footsteps?
In whose torches should we burn?
Whose fireplaces should we warm?

1973

I Hear Them Carrying Quarried Sand from the Sand Pit

Hearing them carry quarried sand
I wake up, go to the window
Where the birch's light-grey
Looks into my room.

When bright sky shines so blue,
What breaks the silence?

Horror's knowledge
Penetrates the heart's dark bulk.

Did they only dig the quarry for us,
Did we lie down there alone,
Didn't mother Russia soothe me,
Cry when the ground did?

1956

At Joy's Summit

The Devil:
How beautiful – the layers of ice below
Where a hundred thousand colours fuse into white,
And here, above where there's a warm valley
Which lifts spring on her shoulders
Like a grandfather lifts a laughing grandson,
A sweet load which heartens
Eh?

God:
Yes, I love Elbrus.

The Devil:
Its unity of smell, sound, colour,
Its limits, its space,
Which you've always known,
My soul craves,
No wonder someone who lived here
Called this mountain "The Summit of Joy"

God:
Adam?

The Devil:
Maybe the half-savage tribes
Learned the vague legends
Of the world's joyful pictures
Before harsh rocks,
Steep cliffs, gloomy gorges,
Where ripe fruit shone everywhere –
Perfumed lemon, whitened apricots,
And grape vines grew with the travellers' joy,
The palm's umbrellas.

God:
Adam got here.

The Devil:
When you threw him out of heaven?

God:
When power sinned for the first time.

The Devil:
He was angry as a child, not knowing,
The rigour of ascent was hard
In heaven he'd been used to plateau.

God:
He got help.

The Devil:
Argued,
Grieved, I approached him,
Breathed pride into him,
But I raged when I saw
Someone who hurts innocents
You, senseless deity,
Standing by his side.

God:
I pitied him.

The Devil:
And tore out of Eden?
He exhausted himself
And you sweetly stroked his eyes –
Explain then why you walked by my side,
To help him?

God:
I loved him.
And you did too at that hard juncture.

The Devil:
Pity, love , easy verbs!
You enraged me
Not because you betray me
But because you lie badly
And still people find your lies sweet.
Why did you love Adam, for power?
Lions are stronger. For weakness? A doe's weaker.
For his utterance? But to you, so long in this world,
A nightingale's probably sweeter.
For his beauty? I see a smile in your eyes –
Admit your whim, mistake, folly, fiction.

God:
Admitted.

The Devil:
Did you say admitted?
Old friend, give me your hand again,
Let's talk, at least once,
Like two students who shared their home,
One may succeed, the other fail
But wealth, honour, fame and poverty's shackles
Give way to warm, urgent dialogue
In a quick day of brief meeting.

God:
Man detached us
Caused this senseless
Ongoing rift
We used to talk.

The Devil:
Weren't we drawn here,
To Elbrus, in the dreaded hour of decay
To try to see, understand
Didn't we decide to meet?

God:
Yes, I sought you out, come, speak,
Be serious. You, like them, ask me the
Same question stubbornly.
What did you love Adam for?
What did you love Adam for?
Didn't he destroy the souls
We now fill with so much detritus and shame?

The Devil:
We enjoyed the taste
Of feral bliss
Didn't want to understand existence
Or the road to perfection.

God:
You've reminded me vividly of the past
When the almost motionless mirror-circles
We saw as we bent over a lake
Framed our reflections with leaves,
We were strange, sudden, identical images.

The Devil:
Your eyes looked more cheerful then.

God:
Yours were thoughtful, languid
And I thought you wiser.

The Devil:
I thought you were the brave one.

God:
And the world, vast, infinite
Which we'd known from outside,
I saw now in you, you in me,

The Devil:
Did we work or play
At making birds, animals,
Flowers, trees, ocean life?
They immediately promptly
Then died.

God:
We were surprised
When they arrived, and by their short lives,
Death remained, as it is, a mystery.

The Devil:
Our brilliant minds were weak,
Devoid of sense and purpose,
We couldn't imagine what good or evil
Would flesh out and clothe our visions,
We were already powerless
Whether we agreed or not,
To exalt or overcome.

God:
They liked us then, knew
No fear, joy, or sorrow,
Power, weakness,
Courage, humility.
Ate herbs and roots,

A tigress sometimes fed a lamb
Or calf – without seeing them as prey.

The Devil:
Until Adam arrived.

God:
I remember the valley's colours that day,
You couldn't stop looking at the flowers,
"I'll make a peacock" you said,
And he immediately appeared,
A toy of nature, a live flower garden,
And for a moment I experienced envy
Your ingenuity engendered it.
It seemed to me a marvel of inspiration.
But, you know I'm honest with you,
Then I thought innovations endless,
Zebra, ostrich, camel,
And since the world neither starts nor ends,
Likeness is better than difference,
Greatness lies in the ordinary,
So I created a third twin,

The Devil:
The same and different,
Everything in him was so close to us – but so new,
He was alien and familiar – this passion
For game, slander, intrigue,
For warm, if late remorse,
For blessing, cursing, crying, laughing senselessly
And by turn, for being open, masked,
Proud, miserable, for spinning secret snares of deceit,
For exciting jealousy in us,
Then changing trickery to cordiality suddenly
Did we have all this in us?

God:
Who knows? Perhaps in his bitterest hour
We first discovered ourselves in him.

The Devil:
Our simple hearts were shocked
When he tore a white sheep to pieces,
Ate it, then stroked the lambs
Guilty, the tears rolled down his face.

God:
Those were the universe's first tears,
You admired their priceless moisture
And he drew closer to you.

The Devil:
No, no, I called out in rage!

God:
Because daily you cared
More for him?

The Devil:
And was jealous
I couldn't stand it
When he listened to you, childish, adoring;
I hated the star,
That covered you both in light.

God:
You were wrong. He loved, believe me,
Two twins equally, couldn't tell us apart,
Any more than he can now.

The Devil:
But you, who suffered as I did,
Told him that he was your creation.

God:
Told him, but later in rage
Because I, like you, was angry, jealous.
I saw our Eden changed by man,
Our flower garden turned into a menagerie.
Adam, by a miracle, somehow noticed,
The obscure features of paradise's nurslings
In rare, dark, moments
And grasped their evil outright,
Told the leopard its law was cruel,
Told the lion its strength,
Told the tree to choke the grass,
Told the grass to fight with numbers,
Saying you are the kingdom,
Told the sheep, you're born victims,
Told the frog, you're ugly,
Told the rose, you're a temptress,
And in him we saw with fright
The seething mass of all these.
We wanted to heal him,
But we too suffered now,
Light, dark, good, evil had been revealed
Entangled us in the roots of our creation.
Century ceded to century
And we said death is evil, life is goodness,
And what happened, to those who valued life most,
Sought evil, wasn't afraid of death's abyss,
Said, I'm dust and will die,
They reached God through a straight gate,
And our useless experience kept on saying,
Light is good, dark is the source of the evil,

But that thought didn't console.
Dark appeared to triumph
Although light flared in human hearts,
Sometimes the powerful light of knowledge blazed
While acts of evil were committed in the dark.
Do you remember the start of suffering,
After the first sin was born
And eternal war ensued?

The Devil:
Between us.

God:
Between everybody,
In everything, in you, in me.
I thought life in Eden became hell
And that war had to be stopped
So I said to man, go away.
But who'd entrusted him to me,
Am I Adam's, everyone's superior?
So I committed the original sin,
Was wrong, punished an equal,
God has no power over his creation,
Although I drove Adam from Paradise,
I couldn't expel him from my heart,
Neither could you, we've matured with him,
We'd been senselessly cruel and senselessly kind,
Walked on, perceived him in new worlds,
Failed to understand the goal,
Saw scaffold and bonfire,
Heard the scream of raid,
The wisdom of freedom's loving whisper,
The soft grumble of maternal tears,
Until the anguish and fear's bitter experience
Brought us to truth's revelation

That evil is bondage and good is freedom.
Let's join the secret police,
Their appearance and nature aren't masked
The investigator wipes sweat from his face,
The face of violence,
Using a drenched handkerchief.
Ruptures a victim's tendons
Transforms a body into a silent wad
With deepest half-blinded eyes
In which there's freedom.
I'm happy because I know year by year,
Day by day, instant by instant,
The menace of the ancient beast of bondage
Loses the charm of power, believe me,
He may roar, but when he peers out of his hole
He's captivated freedom's timid radiance.

The Devil:
You're happy because so far Adam's descendants
Praise you with loud hymns
Even if they deny you, it's me who ruins their souls,
Leads them into the dark.

God:
How do you know what you are,
What I am, that you're not glorified,
The image they use for Christ or Buddha
That you're not their source of kindness?
A shepherd stands with his herd,
When a train thunders the spirit freezes,
But a train can stand still,
A shepherd can dart away,
Brother, dear brother, does it matter,
Which of us is good, light, just think?

The Devil:
My answer has to be sad,
Human will has made my soul
Sullen, shallow, I live
As an inconsequential sinner,
I trust neither smile, tear,
Maternal kiss nor cleansing storm,
Only once when the Atlanteans split the atom,
And changed the world, exploded,
Filled the earth's sphere with fire,
Neutrons, gamma rays,
Dazzled, flashed dazzling, danced,
As seas, wind, rain and snow storms
Became solid, frozen, numbed,
And mountain ridges melted.
As we watched from a buzzing height
Breathless, we trembled terrified,
How the chain advanced,
Decayed all of life, joined us
After thousands of years
And we hugged for the first time,
Clung to each other
Like children in a bomb shelter – you remember, God,
How the avalanche of light calmed down,
The moon's horn shimmered,
We looked at the land without recognition,
Where cornfields and gardens rustled,
Temples and palaces towered,
Men had laboured in factories, railways,
Lay sheets of arctic ice
The lush region of mothers and children
Laboratories, camps, gas stoves, the carefree,
Now wore permafrost,
There was only ice and storm,
Darkness and death unlimited,

Where wild men in animal skins
Had known hard lives,
Mountains rose now and water fell,
But still timidly, shoots emerged,
Men glanced at cloudless light vaults,
Into lake mirrors, quiet rivers,
The new world, its free bloom,
Which seemed to have entered its first century
When we'd live in peace
Neither happy nor sad,
Simple endless days,
Here on Elbrus, where vines had died,
Colour had been lost to ice,
And for the first time after long, dark years
We cried as one and believed you and I
For a short, sweet moment that life would change
Into eternal beauty.

God:
We were wrong.
Where there's good, there's evil,
That's the universe's simple truth.

The Devil:
Everything goes on like before
And our old enmity divides us.
Maybe a chain reaction
Will move the earth's plates again one day
I hope so and this time
Perhaps without light or regrowth.

God:
No, we should rely on light,
Good can't exist without evil
Or destroy evil's power

But I believe I see evil weaken –
Good slowly multiply
I dreamed I'd conquer dark with light
I've got a new faith in me
Dark and light have their measure,
And measure's above all,
For violence to limit,
Obstacles to fall in their thousands,
Bright, wide, freedom to be affirmed,
We must wait and hope.

The Devil:
I hope, brother.

1955

A Literary Memoir[90]

Maybe it's because
I never dared write this in my mind,

Or because the sky came closer
And out of mercy sent someone to listen,

Or because I understood the old year,
And didn't argue with its departure,

Or because the city and the suburbs,
Merge here,

There's always
Car exhaust,

Or because here where I was young
And now hurry to you along the sunset,

And the planet's orbit is disrupted
The firmament rises in two levels,

On top seems to be a lake
Where an aircraft's hull bathes its sail,

Below, a red-fingered hand,
Stops the cloud

So the magical, unbounded, dualistic world
Shines inside me so that beyond the car

I see another winter
Before these houses were built,

With modern ideas
In the years of pettiness and lies,

(We all suffer
Time's subversion of ideas)

I remember a good-shaped crowd
Of newly-planed, five-walled peasant huts,

Some neighboured
Dense, urban buildings.

I remember a pharmacy, a red brick barn
Close to the station.

A cross, seen through darkened space
Like a martyr ascending to the stake

Above the temple which had just been sentenced to close
By the Inter-district Party's meeting.

Nest boxes, a well, beehives
And the silenced song

Of the bells, which all told me
What would break out in the suburbs.

I look around slowly
Absorbed, for the first time, in the entirely Russian scene.

You wouldn't recognize your current friend
In that southern young man,

Were my features odd,
Vain as them, lusted for self sacrifice?

Were they ignorant, erudite, blabbing,
Stubborn, hotheaded?

My compatriot[91] led me to this work,
He saw himself as a reveller,

Carefree, dissolute, a vagrant
Who lived among homeless singers, birders.

And look, I turned into an expert on armies[92],
The cavalry, a fraud, you'll laugh.

It wasn't hard for that tall man
With his woman-slight shoulders,

And a broad, grey forehead,
That artist, my mentor in word-craft,

A pygmalion[93]
Who's grey-green eyes flashed,

Who created his own image
But made no idol of himself,

Squeezed the Jew out of himself[94]
With a fever for the romance of action,

Guns, the whistle hunters' lures,
The longboats' tarred lines.

Everything he'd looked for in great books
He found was in the People's Commissar's
                  and Brigade Commanders

Tachankas[95], leather jackets, obfuscation.
He injected himself with it like an addict,

Or recited the proletariat's glory
Like a frantic, spellbound shaman,

Until the ninth wave[96] of the wild riot,
Opened his eyes,[97]

His vision suddenly healed,
And saw the sorry Ukrainian grain farmer

Tossed between Makhno[98] and military requisitions,
And this nightingale who'd sung in a newsprint cage

Squeezed and chilled his heart
So his pure, rare voice,

Innate, sonorous,
Although wheezed and grunted,[99]

Read poems wherever he found himself,
Joked, "Asthma I can cope with,

Reading Mandelstam aloud
Always helps."

How the tones of his south-western accent,
Carried a rhyme

Sluchevsky, Khodasevich, Kluyev, Blok
In those stalled days

When he sat like a lazy Saracen
And heard my invective

Mocked my youth,
Became indignant and said, "Nonsense" often,

(Responded to my doggerel
The same way),

I once took my poems to a journal
Where he worked, keen to avoid nepotism

I gave them to a secretary
And what did my elder comrade scrawl on them?

"To the 'Diocesan Gazette'" I stayed away
For two days

Then he came to see me in my cubby hole
Asked if I'd gone mad,

Said, "Read this." I did,
Man is weak after all,

"Artful but crowded with the
Faith, freedom etc., a madman,

Good ear, weak eye,
Sometimes draws clearly.

Write from the navel, the gut,
To hell with the childish, banish the muse,

Let it march away with the rest of the country."
The childish? In nineteen twenty one

The oil lamps barely smouldered, we'd starved,
While women from Moldavian villages,

Traded in mony and malay[100],
Cathedrals burned, churches froze,

It was like Eden, there was no work,
At night the gates were locked,

Square peepholes were hacked out
No one unknown was welcome

Residents stood guard with rifles,
Afraid or aggressive.

A funny man made friends with me,
He bought saccharine

Floated tea in hot water,
Made oil cakes in a rumynka[101]

Told me about a gallery opening
He'd been to in Paris,

And beautiful ballerinas
He'd known when he was rich,

The castor sugar, wool, merengo, cheviot,
He'd traded at Leikack Brothers. An older son

Who'd despised trade since childhood,
Lived on an inheritance while it lasted,

Called himself an aesthete,
Dressed fashionably even when devastated,

Looked epicurean.
His father spoke Yiddish, so as not to be understood,

Reminded his mother
That their son's mistress had left him

On the day the officers ran off to Istanbul.
He'd traded morning coats and valises

For bread and peeled barley,
Squeezed into the market crowds.

Late one evening two men came to our home,
Claimed our surplus,

My father showed his Menshevik card
As if he didn't know the risks,

They read RSDRP[102],
Took nothing,

Told my friend to get dressed
Took him away silently. Odesa, childhood,

A shot in that cold February night,
The run to where he lay in the yard

By the gate, our stammerer-janitor, Nikita,
Angry, his mutter,

His lighter held up to the coat,
Who was inside? What? Nothing.

Blood thickening on its sealskin revere,
Eyes which said nothing.

But the janitor always mutters death
Inside me. That won't die,

Maybe I'm real
Because it won't.

I told him [Bagritsky] about nineteen twenty-one,
The shot, "Aesthetes are bitches,

There's a law for the worthy,
You kill those you ought to."

(Later in this poem he'll be even firmer,
More emphatic on this law).

He wanted to be CheKa-like
Mysterious, acute,

Like Blumkin[103], who Gumilyov
Described so well,

As the Imperial Ambassador's assailant,
Who hot on anonymous instructions

Romantic though forensic,
Bagritsky loved the story's power.

That winter he was suddenly caught up
By history of the [National] Convention[104]. He often read

The maxims of Saint-Just[105] and Marat[106] aloud,
In hoarse rhythm

And in the French I heard
Current pain, Russian fear.

That winter had already seen the birth of anxiety,
Like his friends, he thought a lot

About the person wrapped in a carpet,
And sent to Alma Ata under guard.[107]

Turgenev's "On the Eve"[108] describes
The violet horizon behind the limes

Where important Bolsheviks lived
In riverside cottages,

We walked to one by the shortest route,
Through the fields I think, (I've forgotten),

Saw black houses far away, at first
I took the trees for peasant huts.

Nature looked at us, silent.
A dog jumped, then stopped

With wolf-like mistrust. Time had stopped
Long ago. The peasants

Seemed unaware of The Great Break[109]
Land was still a family estate

And even St George's Day[110]
Hadn't arrived there,

The villages had lain in snow for centuries,
While outsiders like us wandered across the fields,

With only the trains' stubborn routines,
As reminders of the twentieth century

Which broke tradition, faith, right
With the arrogance of a bone-setter.

We were headed for a visit.
He [Bagritsky] brought me as company for the way back,

The long frosty night would be harsh,
He waxed about, "The Putilov worker[111]

Party man, loyal to the machine,
CC instructor[112],

Whose wife's one of us[113], from Odesa,
My friend." As we arrived

At a two story wooden house,
Only later did Party leaders get mansions,

Once they'd spilled our guts
And their own.

The mistress of the house answered the door herself
What can I see now in that distant past?

Power, ease,
A chiffon dress,

Weighted, curves,
Slim legs,

Eyes, thick set, snub nosed,
That Great Russians[114]love,

Amber on the over-convex breast,
Party and Art speak.

A fairy tale come true,
Rotted with camp[115] dust.

And beyond the dreams of rag wearers,
Canapés on the ancient regime's occasional tables

Time on one of their grandfather clocks
This too became dust, fiction.

The home cooked meal, all Russian
Except for the radish with pork rinds

A vodka decanter
Gilded inside with lemon peel,

Mirth saying, "I love backwoods,"
The strange arrival of her husband,

As if from nowhere
Was this imagined or intuited?

He was a freak. A sorcerer-freak!
Dwarfish. His mouth crammed,

With mismatched teeth, requisitioned
From different mouths, like the wandering glass eyes

They gave to Lance-Corporals.
He drew up sharp at the window

With his back to us,
For some reason, stood before night's silent dark,

Putting his forehead against the glass,
Turned round, invited us to the table,

Proposed the toast, "So we're neighbours,"
And said nothing more.

While his wife and the poet remembered the South,
The gifted circle of the Green Lamp[116]

Then the reading began. Bagritsky with spirit,
Whistled, rang, clacked, thundered,

Our hostess glanced with her eyes
To come and admire but our ghoulish host

Just asked in the crudest of tones,
"I'd like to know what you think you are,

Border guard or smuggler?
It's clear you're stylish, eloquent."

Who could imagine we were in a demon's lair,
That the bow-legged freak,

The poor moron was Satan,
In those mittens[117] death would be sharpened,

And that a whole impoverished, damned people
Would be terrified by the name of Yezhov?[118]

Pity this man, no devil, no sorcerer,
But a petty departmental clerk, tell tale, snoop.

By what miracle, what power,
Seven years on, did he, scant of mind and will,

Force minions, leaders,
Scientists, the luminary, heroes, rebels

To rot in cesspits as outcasts of reason?
It's a hard and frightening question.

We left on foot. Night, buildings, yards,
Kept their black silence in the snow.

From the blanched heights of frosted air,
Remote worlds shone, lights down,

Pines stood before the princess-winter
Like archers, and my companion,

Who disliked emotional outbursts,
A wit, who mocked like all southerners,

Stooped, grabbed me with his arm,
Put his cheek, wet with tears and snow,

Awkwardly to mine.
Did God's light wake for a moment

In the blind? Or was the blizzard to come,
Foreseen in the poet with a pigeon's eye?

1974

Moldavian is a Language

Moldovan is a language
Which hauls in the dark
Until the last of sunset's banished
By its rugged horse and cart.

Can you hear the swagger,
Of its coppery verbs
The Latin of a convict's dagger
Not the Senate's words?

The Capitol's heights have crumbled
Its artefacts lie low
Only the Dniester's windblown grumble
Keeps the Roman known.

The songs of desperate outlaws
Snipe at the words of the ruler
Clatter once they've stopped their chores
At night beyond the Vorkuta.

To earn a bit more dinner
A puff of a cigarette,
The shivering political sinner
Is singing aloud and yet

His Ovid is adapted here
Crude but still astute
Don't segregate yourselves
For fear of thief or prostitute,

Desperation makes us equal
As we sing and speak
We each contain the sequel
To the other's pique.

Mamalyga and wine at dawn
Give courage to my gullet
And my words are more than brawn
As short lived as a bullet.

One day you'll all be literature
I've read The Almighty's Book
That's why I had to come here
To know, to listen, to look.

1962

Dogs

The bolts screwed tight
So it'll never open again
Laika's[119] gone into orbit
In our airtight box.

She'd been sad when she'd looked at the grass
And strange road signs,
She hadn't known she was a fool
Who'd come to intelligent-dog-land.

She can see now; gardens, palaces,
The Academy's austerity,
The four-legged granite-sage[120]
Celebrated in Red Square.

Politicians, priests, mummers,
Dog-scientists, healers,
Had all rushed[121]
To meet the cross-breed.

Medals had glinted
As the crowed watched their Zhuchka[122]
Her primitive bark
Had shamed and upset them.

What do you know, Commanders,
About the stars in the Golden Dog[123],
Heaven's suffering
Immeasurable and infinite?

What do you say at home
About directives on rickets,
Komi's expanses[124],
Taiga's[125] sovereignty?

Rank's ignoble
Without affinity,
Freedom's nugatory
When friends are chained.

What's the use of thought soaring cloudward
To the logomachy of good and bad
When hearts feel fear and contempt
For their dumb, mad sister?

1957

Do We Need the Colour of a Gypsy Band?

Do we need the colour of a gypsy band,
Verbal-carnival, contrivance,
Fists of fresh epithets
Or metaphors?

If only four of the lines
I write in my old age
Could become prayers
In our horrible world

And be spoken by a priest, in a temple's relic,
To the grey-haired and the young,
Who'd repeat them, after him,
With their lips and their hearts.

1984

The Silent

You're right of course,
The deeper the sadness
The quieter it is.
That's why the forest
Seems like a big confessional,
A place to whisper.

The pine, the oak
Have endless ways to suffer
But not one to describe suffering.

We in our wars and peace
Multiply the fumes of speech;
Complaints, confusion, curses
Live among the sensitive plants,
We howl and scream and swear
And they keep silent.

1963

Sunday Morning in the Forest

Grasshoppers where did you hide until morning,
In the straw hut?
And weren't you the silversmiths,
Who made earrings for the herbs?
The Hanseatic Union of rookeries is a panoply,
The forests' creatures, plants, workshops,
Bush handicrafts leave me unafraid
Of my shadow or anyone else's.
Early evening's chimes call invisibly,
Birds and leaves became more lively
Like craftsmen heading for the cheerful arches of a tavern,
Blades of grass twist like lips
Commenting or jibing sharply,
And an oak talks about their secret society
With a young seamstress-birch.

1970

Fantasy

I also learned how to grind doggerel
Like the modern masters and this
Fades in the even light
Of diurnal need, want, flesh,
But I know I've walked on the planet
Where angels were the only two-legged flesh.
In a dense glade
Pale fawns,
With outlines as flat as horses',
Conversed,
While the bright play of faded colour
Took my vision
And strengthened or lit
My insight.

I began to feel the bliss of awareness
Of birds, nests, waves, planes,
The bare perception of a butterfly's shadow,
That the hieroglyphs plants wear,
Are neither sign, signal, nor vision
But real, substantive.
That those who died by the will of Providence
Returned by it to life,
But to life metaphysical, strange,
Without passion, desire,
Not life subverted,
But elevated,
Where angels as beautiful as animals
Nest in brooks,
Revelations, myths, beliefs,
Don't move through or past them,
But converse with each insight,
In the live cuneiform
Of beings unique in image and visage.

I didn't expect to be parted so soon
From all I've seen here and that's why
I saw so little. I noticed something strange
About angels, they seemed afraid,
Gomorrah-like,
In those caper-strewn, almond-blossomed,
Loutish streets
Where grasshoppers grew heavy,
And forbidden desire lit women's gazes
And men's. Anxious and languid,
They drew their wings to hide their legs
And sweet, awkward, they waited for the devil,
Who came long ago,
Why were they scared then?

There were neither sinners nor demons
These places were quiet, beautiful,
Their glow was dissolved in daylight
Why were the angels timid,
Hopeless, despondent?
Did they know the demons weren't external
But grew inside them, languished,
Inert, craved the movement
Of minds withered in war,
The smoke of alters covered in the blood of lambs?
How could they live in the bit of that fire?

They hadn't looked at me, they'd been stunned
Thrown by the Almighty into this terrible world,
To them I'd looked incongruous,
Meanwhile I'd been drawn
To the limp omnipotence of light and shade,
Magic glass,
Splinters of forgotten images.

This is what I saw,
Neither bodies nor action,
But Austrian soldiers laughing,
A Croat undiscouraged by captivity,
A yard-keeper's badge and broom.
My memory's a shaft of light
Which shows me the friends I had when I was young,
Coherent, intelligent, statelessness,
Life in midnight rail carriages,
Suburban cold at the windows,
Shattered Moscow's train stations,
Prison camps, a drive in the Moldavian woods
Where I first learned the language of the grass
Which is more complex than poems, chess,
The way people smell, languish,
Then dig ditches for themselves.
A light-brown haired head
And fluently-arrogant grin
Are aways with me[126],
Another irascible, spendthrift,
Sweet-toothed sad poet[127] had that grin

I can still see the tailor's sign,
It offers to hem, sew, gofre and accordion pleats,
The embroiderer had no time for Greens[128]

Whites, Petlyra[129] – Budyonny[130]
The cavalry, infantry or navy,
CheKa were, "Robbers who loot",
Only a Tsar, "Keeps you safe!"
Are you here as well Monsieur Degtyar?[131]
No, you've truly been killed off.
You thought that it was safer
In the charnel house waiting for the Germans,
In the countryside near half a dozen huts

Far from the sea, heat plenty of food
In the steppe's sand, thyme, tarragon, poppy,
The German's cultured, not tramps,
If it has to be a ghetto
Is that worse than this?
Oh God of vengeance and of the covenant,
Make all of this perish.

And then, as now, it was the end of summer,
And then, as now, it was quiet,
But the land was enveloped in a different silence,
Everything that was something
Became nothing, grass, sand, smile, sigh,
The city seemed struck dumb, deaf,
And for many families time
Stood still forever. Imperceptibly,
Seemed to ebb, like pity,
And what did everyone say to themselves, each other,
During the long countryside nights?
Do the lucky among victims
Become torturers?
Without being betrayed,
They went to the police themselves,
As though led by curse or sorcery
To defy order, decree, rule,
They first went to Preobrazhenskaya[132]
Then turned downhill into Kherson[133]
Where the charming town became a non-Russian stranger,
Smelled of almost sural expanse and estuaries.
My mother was left behind,
When they went to their dachas
They said there was no room,
Beside she was made of different dough,
So they lay, shot, in the pit without her
But she's with them now,

Cool, different, unearthly.[134]

Was it the kind, grey, big-eyed acacia in our yard
Or my mother's voice I heard?
"Shall I close the door?
No, not this one, – not this one son.
What's my grave in Vostryakovskya like?
No, no the worlds' not nothing son,
It's us, we're in all of it, all of it's in each of us.
You're finally in love, for the first time?
It took you long enough, congratulations,
Did this one resemble me?
Was that what made the difference?"
I touched the white flowers,
"Love is God, how can God be loved
For the last or first time?"
I remembered what I'd tried to forget,
I hadn't fallen in love, but returned to it.

1974

Thrush

A half-savage river
Courses from the sky,
Drowns the roar of plants,
The hum of trucks,

While Xerxes' Macedonian henchmen
Watch its current,
And cavalry footfall
Fades in distant mist.

But the huge rage
Of the movement's thunder
Can't block out the small thrush

His simple-hearted pride
Seems unaware
It argues with the river gorge.
Doesn't know what it sings

About today and the future,
While the river trembles
As it keeps pace with the bird song
That inspired its tremble.

1965

In the Desert

We move in the fourth dimension
Like pilgrims with sublime humility.
Haze then whirlwinds shot up
In the sandstorms of time's desert,
Tall cranes loom
Over daydreamed centuries.

We visit our pasts,
So our grandchildren can dream
Our forebears' stories,
We think we wander in the same places
But we find new ones
When we travel without a goal.

The pioneer is always forgotten.
What does he enjoy on his way?
A well here in the sand and heat
Where you feel time as freedom
As you drink stagnant water
From the eternal bucket.

1978

By the Sea

The waves crashed under the flicker of the lighthouse
And I, in my ignorance, heard a monotone.
Years later the sea speaks to me and I begin to understand
There are birds and laundresses, sprites and sorcerers
Laments and curses, moans and profanity, white horses
And half-breeds who rear up unexpectedly.
There are waves who are salesgirls with buxom hips
Who sell foam from the counter, they tremble fluid or airy.
Nature can't be indifferent, she always mimics us
Like a loan, a translation; we're the blueprint she's the copy.
Once upon a time the pebble was different
And so the wave was different.

1965

In the Daytime

Someone marks a flat vale with black sheep and dogs
Burned and bitten by the sun and sand.
They create a language I try to read.

I've forgotten about the slate and tin
Of a dusty settlement in the steppe.
What if I could learn this wedge writing?
But its meaning is hidden, unknowable.

1984

When I Was Putting Letters into Words

And helping their meaning along,
I had a sense of how my life would go,
I wouldn't ever grow tall enough
To close window vents, I'd champ at the bit,
Die with the face of an ordinary, frightened man,
The crazy age would raise its batons
Against my rebellious passivity.

But my life was mysterious, with a strange understanding
Of metaphysical truth in the creative world,
And if I despaired, from the all-victorious breakdown,
I found joy in repentance and my weakness gave me strength.

1976

Tao

Break the chain of emotion, passion,
Cleanse the blood of desire,

Turn your body into a trunk,
Your heart to ash,

But the ash must be devoid of sap,
The ash of spark,

Forget this world, path,
Your very self.

1962

Two Mirrors

Powder makes your face strangely young,
Curling irons give your moustache an impressive twirl,
The waves in your greying hair are flattened over your low forehead,
Your eyes darken, convex, damp.

Bare nymphs decorate your cane handle,
Large diamonds your tie,
Will you, the dead's classmate
Start and end your life a dandy?

Was there an ache however brief or small,
Of sharp anxiety in your barren soul
On a cold morning,
In a rearguard blizzard?

Did the torment of war really school you
In selfish fear, bitter stasis
Wasn't even a single kernel of pain's beauty
Logged in your dry breast?

In the next chair a thin, sad, boy
Just off a train from the battlefield
Who's left his suitcase in a locker
And dozed off under the razor's gentle scrape

Without recognising the barber
As a friend he'd dreamt up
From the peace of his still-recent childhood
A prayer, longing, spouse.

Isn't that who he prays he'll dream of
Not as she is but with her long braid
And the flutter of her lashes
Before their mascara is washed away with tears.

179

1944

Time

Didn't Isaiah shout in front of me
That the Covenant was undermined in filth,
Didn't blind Aoidos recite poems
In front of me that shook the Achaeans?

As we move from the cradle to the grave,
Don't we feel the world move? We're still,

But the living and those who've lived,
We're all close. What's the past,

What we call now, tomorrow?
They define nothing
Death is something we won't pass,
Time is what's dead in memory.

And more than once I've been surprised
By how nothing's divided from us by years;
The Angel in the Apocalypse swore
That time would disappear forever.

1975

The Monkey House

When the beginning of time
And sacred books were forgotten
Our reluctant forebears
Saw robbery, hunting,

Forfeited household rights
For those of stars, heavens,
Fields, flowers,
Turned slowly to the forests.

The wild grew uneven,
A primate not yet extinct,
Didn't talk but lowed,
No more a beast, already primaeval,

And where decay was fastest,
The uranium fuelled;
Handsome, literate leaders
Became monkey descendents.

As yet I don't need long paws,
But I go into the monkey house,
Feel the acid smell of nitrogen,
Say to the miserable progeny time and again:

"The wreckage of God's kingdom faces you,
Good years ruined.
We, happier descendants,
Go into the darkness after you."

1963

Conversation

Her voice was sweet her laughter gentle,
Wasn't she my pernicious sin?

Her gentle sweetness of hers was given by Me,
She isn't your pernicious sin.

I blazed with desire for ghostly glory
Wasn't my sin that I wanted fame?

I Myself lit that desire in you,
A prophet blazes with his clear flame.

I've always valued gold vanity,
Was it my sin that I lived prosperously?

You always liked gold fuss
It's not the sin I deem the worst.

I played with words, created them,
Should my head be blamed?

You didn't create words but yourself,
I who spoke with every word you used.

I believed in Thee, and didn't,
Am I a sinner in that I destroyed my spirit?

Leaving Me, you came to Me,
And losing Me, you found Me.

I was a bowl of sins, some I can't remember,
What then was my worst, most heinous sin?

You have seen how gloom pretends to radiate
But in dark you saw the divine.

You have seen how deception pretends to be truth
Why did you let your soul be penetrated?

Yes, you didn't go to war on the black evil,
Why did it then crawl into your mind?

Yes, you were cunning with the world and with the crowd,
But tell me why you are cunning with yourself?

Why you don't even tell the whole truth,
To yourself, why?

You don't tell yourself what you hid from everyone
This is your terrible sin, your heinous sin.

But O God, when will I be shriven?
When the time comes and when I converse.

1942

Two Nights

The world has seen many storms
But the worst and most terrible
Were those two between God's death
And the Resurrection.
And the horror was that no-one,
No-one noticed during those nights
That the world became crueller,
Shallow, pettier.
Camel bells tinkled,
Distant fires smouldered,
But the dead God didn't cry
In the local, ancient language,
Populations kept growing –
Things multiplied –
I, like you, was born
During one of those two nights.

1962

ENDNOTES

1   Quoted by Solzhenitsyn as, "I, terrified of prison … / Am threatened by the very people / Who reject the laws of man" It may be that Lipkin gave or recited from memory a different version of this poem to Solzhenitsyn.

2   This poem concerns the fate that befell Lipkin's friend, the poet Anna Akhmatova; the death of her husband Nikolai Gumilyov and the imprisonment of their son Lev. In the final stanza, Lipkin reverses the idiom "bylo, da splylo", it was but swam away, (disappeared), to hint that past horrors such as those suffered by Akhmatova still pervade Soviet life.

3   Peasant, literally a mature man (Russian)

4   The nickname party members used for Stalin

5   Land forming part of the Russian Federation situated east of the Kama river's left bank which stretches up to the Urals where there used to be Gulag camps.

6   In Tsarist Russia prisoners feet were shackled.

7   Siberia's first settlers and their descendents.

8   1930's Soviet jeep.

9   Druzhba – "friendship", a Soviet make of motor-saw

10   Kulaks

11   Violin, one of the main traditional musical instruments of the Abkhazians.

12   The Revolutionary Committee.

13   Both forbidden to her by Islam (Translator's Note).

14   Georgian's i.e. Stalin's.

15   A member of Tsar Ivan the Terrible's (Grozny) (1530 – 1584), secret police, the tool by which he purged Russia's nobility.

16   Central Executive Committee.

17   Grigory Zinoviev 1883-1936, head of the Comintern for many years. He was found guilty in the so-called 'Trial of the Sixteen' and was thus executed.

18   Lev Kamenev 1883-1936, Soviet Russia's first head of State. Acted as premier in the last years of Lenin's life. He was found guilty in the so-called 'Trial of the Sixteen' and was thus executed.

19   Karl Radek 1885-1939, Comintern secretary until his removal in 1923. He was later expelled from the party and then readmitted. In 1937, he was found guilty in the so-called 'Trial of the Seventeen' and thus sentenced to ten years penal labour. It was established during the 'Khrushchev Thaw' that he was killed by an NKVD operative.

20   Mikhail Tomsky 1880-1936, led the All-Russian Central Council of Trade Unions. He killed himself in the early days of 'The Great Terror' and was tried posthumously.

21 Nikolai Bukharin 1888-1938, General Secretary of the Comintern's executive committee until 1929, though he later lost his position and party membership due to his opposing 'collectivisation'. He was executed.

22 Labourer.

23 "A man who builds production plants based on historical production standards and declares they indicate the limit of production capacity."

24 A lishentes from the Russian word "deprivation".

25 Members of the Alash Orda which attempted to create an independent state in Kazakhstan.

26 Siberia's prehistoric forests.

27 Nestor Makhno (1884-1934), a Ukrainian anarchist revolutionary and the commander of the Revolutionary Insurgent Army of Ukraine during the Ukrainian Civil War.

28 Stalin was born in Gori.

29 (1929-2010), Revolutionary and Marxist theoretician.

30 Georgy Plekhanov (1856-1918), Founder of Russian Marxism.

31 The best brand of Armenian brandy.

32 Georgian term for a man engaged in trade or with no occupation, a humorist, a rogue and a swindler.

33 Abkhaz wine.

34 The end (Georgian colloqu.).

35 Mother (Abkhaz).

36 A Moscow prison.

37 Refers to Vasily Grossman's letter To the First Secretary of the Central Committee of the Communist Party Nikita Khrushchev.

38 Southern Black Sea (modern day Anatolia)

39 The Ministry's Central administrative board (USSR)

40 Seaside coffee house

41 Lykhny — Abkhaz village, known for its beauty and ancient history (mentioned in 6th century AD.).

42 Final church service of the day.

43 "The Great Perm" was a medieval Komi State. Today it is the Russian Federation's "Permkrai".

44 "The Small Perm" was a region of "The Great Perm".

45 Under the Tsars, convicts were punished by having their nostrils torn.

46 A measure of grain (Tsarsirist)

47   Plain clothes.

48   Petty thieves/blokes (Russian criminal's slang).

49   Operupolnomchennyi – secret service operational commissioners who were assigned
      to Soviet institutions both inside and outside labour camps each at least one CheKa/
      GPU/NKVD/KGB representative controlling ideology, (in the Red Army they were called
      commissars).

50   In the manuscript 'ssuchilis'(branch) became 'sukas' (leaf) – prisoners who
      collaborated betraying their fellows, informant colloq.

51   Russia's annual Women's day.

52   Siberia.

53   City in the Perm where sink holes open up.

54   Socialist Revolutionaries – members of a Russian political party persecuted by the
      Bolsheviks after they seized power in October 1917.

55   Quoted by Solzhenitsyn as,"What the victims would have done / If they'd succeeded? /
      Could they have become the executioners?" It may be that Lipkin gave or recited from
      memory a different version of this poem to Solzhenitsyn.

56   Rhymed and metered, ironic, Ukrainian and Russian folk songs.

57   Isiah 40:8.

58   Kibitka – portable dwellings of central Asian nomads.

59   In Odesa's oblast, Ukraine (major railway station on Odesa-Zhmerinka line).

60   A Soviet slogan applied to Kulaks.

61   Novitiate – from 'belyi' white.

62   Nun – from 'chernyi' black.

63   Diminutive for Marina Tsvetaeva.

64   Diminutive for Anna Akhmatova.

65   The Russian Orthodox bake lark pie for Easter.

66   A tsarist Russian free trade zone.

67   Leningrad (now St Petersburg)'s "Our Lady of Kazan" Cathedral.

68   During WW2 there was only one escape route from besieged Leningrad over the ice of
      Lake Ladoga which became known as "The Ice Road to Salvation."

69   Novorossiya – the area north of the Black Sea which was conquered by Tsarist Russia at
      the end of the 18th Century which included Odesa where Lipkin was born.

70   Folk play (Ukrainian) cf rhapsod (Greek)

71   Nomads living in Asia Minor in Seventh Century BCE

72   Playing dominoes (colloq.).

73   The nightingale.

74   In 1919 Admiral Kolchak's White Army was defeated by the Red Army.

75   Russia's Far East

76   Residents of the region since the 18th Century who held Orthodox beliefs that were contrary to those the official Russian church.

77   The name given to members of the religion the Semeiske adhered to.

78   Bolshevik regional committee member.

79   The majority of those who initially served in CheKa were executed in 1937's Great Terror.

80   1969

81   Nobility (Polish)

82   Mr. (Polish)

83   Outer garment worn by Hungarian, Polish, Belorussian, Lithuanian male nobles.

84   Celebrates God speaking to the entire Jewish people at Mount Sinai and Moses bringing the law on the tablets of stone, which together with what God told Moses constitutes the Tora.

85   The handwritten Tora scroll is always cased in velvet in an Ashkenazi's synagogue.

86   Most synagogues have more than one Tora and on the Tora festival they are all brought out of the ark at once.

87   Here Lipkin seems to be adopting a liturgical tone albeit to voice his own sentiment rather than join in that of the congregation he observes.

88   The congregation sing hymns while circling the synagogue seven times carrying their scrolls

89   And – (Yi in Russian) the first syllable of Israel the country, and of a biblical name for the Jewish people.

90   The poem's interlocutor is Edward Bagritsky, the profusely talented first romantic then constructivist poet (1895-1934) who mentored Lipkin from the age of 18.

91   Bagritsky like Lipkin, was born in Odesa.

92   Lipkin was a World War 2 conscript who fought and reported from the Front.

93   The sculptor in Ovid's "Metamorphoses" who fell in love with a statue he carved.

94   A reference to Anton Checkov's statement, "To be free you must squeeze the slave out of yourself."

95   Horse spring wagon's from which mounted machine guns fired during Russia's Civil War. Mythologised in songs and poems.

96   1919 when international revolution hadn't transpired and Trotsky turned his attention to internal resistance in Siberia and South Russia.

97   Bagritsky crossed and re-crossed Jewish, Russian and Soviet boundaries in his highly influential and controversial work.

98   Nestor Ivanovych Makhno was a Ukrainian anarcho-communist revolutionary and the commander of an independent anarchist army in Ukraine during Russia's Civil War (1888-1934)

99   Bagristky died at age 35 from asthma.

100   Pudding made with cornmeal.

101   Makeshift stove used in the famines during the 1920's.

102   Revolutionary Russian Soviet Democratic Labour Party formed in 1898 which Vladimir Ilyich Ulyanov (Lenin) joined prior to 1903.

103   Yakov Blumkin, a legendary CheKist, (1898-1929)

104   French post revolutionary legislature 1792-1795.

105   Louis, Antoine de Saint-Just, French revolutionary military leader (1767-1828)

106   Jean-Paul Marat physician, radical journalist in the French Revolutionary (1743-1793)

107   Verny became Alma Ata under Soviet rule in 1921. Now Almaty, Khazakistan. The identity of this person isn't known by the translators.

108   Penguin Books Ltd., 1950

109   USSR's 1928/9 economic policy turn.

110   Yuriev Day, the week pre and post 16th Century November 26th, when dependent peasants could move fro one owner to another.

111   Initiators of The National Strike of 1905.

112   Central Committee of the Communist Party

113   Both Bagritsky and Lipkin were Jewish.

114   Velikorrsy as opposed to Malorossy (Ukrainians)

115   Gulag

116   Odesa's Literary association (1910-1920).

117   Yezhov derives from yezh, Russian for hedgehog. Russian idiom, "to handle someone with a hedgehog's mittens" means to treat someone harshly. Also see note 179.

118   Nikolai Ivanovich Yezhov was a Soviet secret police official under Joseph Stalin. He was head of the NKVD from 1936 to 1938, during the most severe period of Stalin's Great Purge.

119   A Moscow stray, the first animal to orbit the earth.

120   Lenin's tomb.

121   Sputnik second launch was hurried to commemorate the Revolution's 60th Anniversary.

122   Little Bug. Russian nickname commonly given to dogs.

123   Canis Borealis

124   Where Gulags are numerous.

125   The world's largest Oblast.

126   Translators cannot identify who this is.

127   Mandelstam

128   Green Army, Russian peasant who fought against requisitions or reprisals by all sides in the Russian Civil War.

129   Symon Pelyra, Ukrainian Jewish Separatist (1879-1926)

130   Semon Budyonny, a real Cossack, Stalin's close ally, (1883-1973).

131   Degtyarov machine gun 1928-1960's defunct by the time this poem was composed

132   A Moscow Metro station in the Preobrazhenskoye District, Eastern Administrative Okrug, Moscow opened in 1965.

133   A city in Southern Ukraine.

134   An allusion to Vasily Grossman's mother who predeceased her son when she was shot at Berdichev in 1941. Until his death in 1964 Grossman continued to write to her. His otherwise devoted wife hadn't wanted to bring her to live with them in Moscow when Grossman's mother suggested it.

BIBLIOGRAPHY OF LIPKIN'S WORK

Poetry:

Ochevidets [*Eyewitness: poems of various years*]; Elista: Kalmyk Book Publishers, 1967; 2nd Edition, 1974.

Vechnyi Den' [*Eternal Day*]; Moscow: Sovetsky Pisatel'*, 1975.

Volia [*Free Will*]; selected by Joseph Brodsky. Ann Arbor: Ardis, 1981; Moscow: O.G.I., 2003.

Kochevoi Ogon' [*A Nomadic Flame*]; Ann Arbor: Ardis, 1984.

Kartiny i golosa [*Pictures and Voices*]; London: Overseas Publications Interchange, 1986.

Lira. Stikhi Raznyh Let [*Lyre. Verses of Various Years*]; Moscow: Pravda, 1989.

Lunnyi Svet. Stikhotvoreniya i Poemy [*Moonlight. Verses and Poems*]; Moscow: Sovremennik, 1991.

Pis'mena. Stikhotvoreniya i Poemy [*Letters. Verses and Poems*]; Moscow: Khudozhestvennaia Literatura, 1991.

Pered Zakhodom Solntsa. Stikhi i Perevody [*Before the Sunset. Verses and Translations*]; Paris-Moscow-New York: Tretya Volna, 1995.

Posokh [*Shepherd's Crook*]. Moscow: CheRo, 1997.

Sobranie sochinenia v 4-kh tomakh [*Collected works in 4 volumes*]; Moscow: Vagrius, 1998.

Sem' desiatiletii [*Seven Decades*]; Moscow: Vozvrashchenie, 2000.

Vmeste. Stikhi [*Together, Verses*]; (Together with Inna Lisnyanskaya). Moscow: Grail, Russkiy put', 2000.

Ochevidets [*Eyewitness: selected poems*]; Compiled by Inna Lisnyanskaya. Moscow: Vremia, 2008.

Prose:

The Stalingrad Ship (stories), 1943

Decade (first novel), 1983

Stalingrad of Vasily Grossman, 1984

Life and Fate of Vasily Grossman. Farewell (With Anna Berzer), 1990

The Flaming Coal. Sketches and Discourses, 1991

The Second Road (memoirs), 1995

Blazing Fire (sketches and observations about Georgii Shengeli), 1995

Kvadriga (short fiction and memoirs), 1997

Examples of Translations by Lipkin:

Abkhaz

Bagrat Shikuba, Moi zemlyaki [*My Compatriots, a poem*]; transl. from Abkhaz by S. Lipkin and Ya. Kozlovsky. Moscow, 1967.

Akkadian

Gilgamesh; verse adaptation by S. Lipkin; afterword by Vyacheslav V. Ivanov. St Petersburg: Pushkin Fund, 2001.

Buryat

Geser [*Geser, Buryat Heroic Epos*]; Moscow: Khudozhestvennaia Literatura, 1968

Derzhava rannikh zhavoronkov. Povest po motivam buryatskogo eposa [*The State of Early Skylarks. A novella on the Motives of Buryat Epos*]; a children's version by S. Lipkin. Moscow: Detgiz, 1968.

Dagestani

Dagestanskie liriki [*Dagestani Lyric Poets*]; translations by S. Lipkin and others. Leningrad: Sovetsky Pisatel', 1961.

Kabardian

Shogentsukov, Ali. Poemy [*Poems*]; translated from Kabardian by S. Lipkin. Moscow: Sovetsky Pisatel', 1949.

Narty [*Narts, Kabardian Epos*]; translated by S. Lipkin. Moscow: Khudozhestvennaia Literatura, 1951.

Kabardinskaia epicheskaya poezia [*Kabardian Epic Poetry*]; selected translations. Nal'chik, 1956.

Debet Zlatolikii i ego druzia: Balkaro-Karachaev nartskii epos [*Debet Goldenface and his friends: Karachai-Balkar Nart epic*]; translated by S. Lipkin. Nal'chik: Elbrus, 1973.

Kalmyk

Prikliyucheniya bogatyrya Samshura, prozvannogo Lotosom [*Adventures of Hero Shamshur, Nicknamed Lotus*], a children's adaptation of the Kalmyk epic story by S. Lipkin. Moscow: Detgiz, 1958.

Dzhangar: Kalmytski narodny epos [*Djangar: Kalmyk national epic*]; translated by S. Lipkin. Elista: Kalmyk Book Publishers, 1971, repr. 1977.

Dzhangar: Kalmytski narodny epos; novye pesni [*Djangar: Kalmyk national epic; new songs*]; poetic translations realised by V N Eremenko, S. Lipkin, Yu. M. Neiman. Elista: Kalmyk Book Publishers, 1990.

Kirghiz

Kirgizskii narodnyi epos "Manas" [*Kirghiz Folk Epos Manas*], transl. S. Lipkin and Mark Tarlovsky. Moscow: Khudozhestvennaia Literatura, 1941.

Poety Kirgizii: Stikhi 1941–1944 [*Kirghiz Poets: Verses*

1941–1944]; translated under the editorship of S. Lipkin.
Moscow: Sovetskiy Pisatel', 1946.

Manas Velikodushny: povest [Manas the Magnanimous: a
novella]; (version by S. Lipkin). Leningrad, 1947.

Manas: epizody iz kirgizskogo narodnogo eposa [*Manas:
episodes from the Kirghiz national epic*]; translated by S. Lipkin
and L. Penkovski. Moscow: Khudozhestvennaia Literatura,
1960.

Manas Velikodushny. Povest' o drevnikh kirghizskikh geroyakh
[*Manas the Magnanimous: a Story about Ancient Kirghiz
Heroes*]; Riga: Polaris, 1995.

Sanskrit

Mahabharata (Indian epic). In: series Biblioteka vsem-
irnoi literatury, vol.2, translated from Sanskrit by S. Lipkin.
Moscow: Khudozhestvennaia Literatura, 1969.

Tatar

Poety Tatarii, 1941–1944 [*Poets of Tataria, 1941–1944*]; edited
by A. Erikeeva and S. Lipkin. Moscow: Sovetsky Pisatel', 1945.

*Poeziya Sovetskoi Tatarii: Sbornik sostavlen Soiuzom Sovetskikh
Pisatelei Tatarskoi ASSR* [*Poetry of Soviet Tataria: Collection
compiled by the Union of Soviet Tatar Writers*]; editor S. Lipkin
[translations by various hands].Moscow: Khudozhestvennaia
Literatura, 1955.

Idegei: tatarskii narodnyi epos [*Idegei: Tatar national epic*];
translated by S. Lipkin. Kazan': Tatar Book Publishers, 1990.

Tajik-Farsi

Firdawsi. Skazanie o Bakhrame Chubine [*Epos about Bakhram
Chubin*]; a fragment from poem Shāhnāmah translated
from Tajik-Farsi by S. Lipkin. Stalinabad [Dushanbe]:
Tadzhikgosizdat, 1952.

Izbrannoe [*Selections*]; translated from Tajik-Farsi by V. Levik and S. Lipkin. Moscow, 1957.

Firdawsi. Poėmy iz Shakh-namė [*Poems from Shāhnāmah*]; in translation by S. Lipkin. Stalinabad [Dushanbe]: Tadzhikgosizdat, 1959.

Stranitsy Tadzhikskoy Poezii [*Pages of Tajik Poetry*]; ed. S. Lipkin, Stalinabad [Dushanbe]: Tadzikgosizdat, 1961.

Rudaki, stikhi [*Rudaki, verses*]; transl. S. Lipkin and V. Levik, ed. I. Braginsky. Moscow: Nauka, 1964.

Tetrad' bytiia [*Book of Life*]; Poetry in Tajik dialect with Russian by S. Lipkin. Lipkin. Dushanbe: Irfon, 1977.

Uzbek

Khamid Alimdzhan. Oigul i Bakhtiyor [*Oigul i Bakhtiyor*]; Tashkent: Goslitizdat UzSSR, 1948.

Lutfi. Gul I Navruz [*Gul and Navruz, a poem*]; transl. S.Lipkin. Tashkent: Goslitizdat UzSSR, 1959.

Navoi, Leili i Medzhnun [*Leili and Medjnun*]; poem translated from Uzbek by S. Lipkin. Moscow: Goslitizdat, 1945; Moscow: Detgiz, 1948; Tashkent: Khudozhestvennaia Literatura, 1957; (In: A Navoi. *Poemy* [*Poems*].), Moscow: Khudozhestvennaia Literatura, 1972.

Navoi, Sem' Planet [*Seven Planets*]; poem translated from Uzbek by S. Lipkin. Tashkent, 1948; Moscow, 1954; (In: A. Navoi. Poemy [*Poems*].); Moscow: Khudozhestvennaia Literatura, 1972.

Golosa Shesti Stoletii [*Voices of Six Centuries*]; selected translations from Uzbek. Tashkent, 1960.

Tsarevna iz goroda T'my [*Princess from the City of Darkness*]; children's story by S. Lipkin based on Uzbek tales. Moscow: Detgiz, 1961.

Slovo i Kamen [*Word and Stone*]; selected translations from Uzbek poetry by S. Lipkin, Tashkent: Gafur Gulyam Publ., 1977.

Mixed Language Anthologies:

Stroki Mudrykh [*Lines of the Wise Ones*]; coll. translations by S. Lipkin,Moscow: Sovetskiy Pisatel′, 1961.

O bogatyriakh, umeltsakh i volshebnikhakh [*On Heroes, Craftsmen and Wizards*]; 3 novellas on Caucasian folklore motives, children's adaptation by S. Lipkin. Moscow: Detgiz, 1963.

Zolotaya zep' [*The Golden Chain: Eastern Poems*]; translated from Abkhaz, Tajik-Farsi, old-Uzbek, etc. Moscow: Detgiz, 1970.

Dalekie i Blizkie: Stikhi zarubezhnykh poetov v perevode [*Far and Near: Verses by foreign poets in translation*]; translators: Vera Markova, S. Lipkin, Aleksandr Gitovich. Moscow: Progress, 1978.

Bibliography of Translations of Lipkin's Work

English translations of Lipkin's work:

One poem translated by Yvonne Green, one poem translated by Robert Chandler, in *The Penguin Book of Russian Poetry* by Robert Chandler, Boris Drayluk and Irina Mashinski, Penguin Classics 2015.

Six poems translated by Yvonne Green, 2 poems translated by Daniel Weissbort, in *Cardinal Points*, www.stosvet.net/12/green, 2011

Two poems translated by Amelia Glaser, in *An Anthology of Jewish-Russian Literature Volume 2 1953-2001* edited by Maxim D Shrayer, M E Sharpe Inc, 2007.

Four poems translated by Albert C. Todd, in *Twentieth Century Russian Poetry*, selected with an introduction by Yevgeny Yevtushenko, edited by Albert C. Todd and Max Hayward, with Daniel Weissbort. New York: Doubleday; London: Fourth Estate, 1993.

French translations of Lipkin's work:

Le Destin De Vassili Grossman translated by Alexis Berelowitch, L'Age d'Homme, Lausanne, 1990.

APPENDIX OF VERSIONS, ORIGINAL POEMS, AND THEIR WEB REFERENCES

Most of the following poems appear on Russian language websites where a large selection of Lipkin's poems can be found. Two poems (At Joy's Summit and Fantasy) can be found online on the Hendon Press website at the given URLs.

The Technical Lieutenant-Quartermaster [Техник-интендант]
https://coollib.com/b/146320/read#t96

The Cooperative Of Deaf Mutes [Комбинат глухонемых]
https://coollib.com/b/s146320/read#t76

Ghosts [Призраки]
https://thelib.ru/books/lipkin_semen/ochevidec_izbrannye_stihotvoreniya-read-4.html#TOC_idm3329200

In No Faith, Freedom, Love [В неверии, неволе, нелюбви]
https://coollib.com/b/146320/read#t10

I Bought You My Thoughts [Я принес вам свои раздумия]
https://coollib.com/b/146320/read#t230

Early Summer [Раннее лето]
https://coollib.com/b/146320/read#t42

My Friend [Одна моя знакомая]
https://coollib.com/b/146320/read#t70

This And That [То да се]
https://ruthenia.ru/60s/lipkin/to_da_se.htm

The Taiga [Тайга]
https://coollib.com/b/146320/read#t89

Funeral [Похороны]

https://ruthenia.ru/60s/lipkin/pohorony.htm

Drawing Of A Greek Square [Рисунок на греческой площади]

https://coollib.com/b/146320/read#t81

The Executioner [Палач]

https://www.livelib.ru/quote/2009927-sem-desyatiletij-semen-lipkin

Nestor And Saria [Нестор и Сария]

http://apsnyteka.org/868-lipkin_s_nestor_i_saria.html

Evening in Lykhny [Вечер в Лыхнах]

https://rustih.ru/semyon-lipkin-vecher-v-lyxnax/

Solikamsk in August 1962 [Соликамск в августе 1962 года]

https://iknigi.net/avtor-semen-lipkin/30936-ochevidec-izbrannye-stihot-voreniya-semen-lipkin/read/page-21.html

Chastushka [Частушка]

https://coollib.com/b/146320/read#t85

Moonlight [Лунный свет]

https://coollib.com/b/146320/read#t98

A Hamlet [Деревенька]

https://coollib.com/b/146320/read#t234

A Nook In The Forest [Лесной уголок]

https://coollib.com/b/146320/read#t263

Beggars in 1922 [Нищие в двадцать втором]

https://coollib.com/b/146320/read#t300

The Field Behind The Forest [В поле за лесом]

https://coollib.com/b/146320/read#t279s

On The River Istra [На Истре]
https://coollib.com/b/146320/read#t280

When You Appeared To Me In My Native Town [Когда мне в городе
родном]
https://coollib.com/b/146320/read#t299

Southern Churches [Южные церкви]
https://coollib.com/b/146320/read#t151

Autumn At The Sea [Осень у моря]
https://coollib.com/b/146320/read#t231

A May Night In The Forest [Майская ночь в лесу]
https://libking.ru/books/poetry-/poetry/278812-61-semen-lipkin-bolshaya-
kniga-stihov.html#book

Commissar [Комиссар]
https://coollib.com/b/146320/read#t175s

The Compound at Vilnius [Вильнюсское подворье]
https://coollib.com/b/146320/read#t101

Ashes [Зола]
https://coollib.com/b/146320/read#t126

Moses [Моисей]
https://coollib.com/b/146320/read#t123

Odesa's Synagogue [Одесская синагога]
https://coollib.com/b/146320/read#t141

And [Союз]
https://coollib.com/b/146320/read#t122

Nomads' Fire [Кочевой огонь]
https://coollib.com/b/146320/read#t174

I Hear Them Carrying Quarried Sand From The Sand Pit
[Слышу, как везут песок с карьера]
https://coollib.com/b/146320/read#t278

At Joy's Summit [Беседа на вершине счастья]
https://hendonpress.co.uk/lipkin-poems-from-the-original-russian/#summit

A Literary Memoir [Литературное воспоминание]
https://iknigi.net/avtor-semen-lipkin/30936-ochevidec-izbrannye-stihot-
voreniya-semen-lipkin/read/page-21.html#sel=554:1,557:14

Do We Need the Colour of a Gypsy Band
[Ужели красок нужен табор]
https://coollib.com/b/146320/read#t260

Moldavian is a Language [Молдавский язык]
https://coollib.com/b/146320/read#t90

Dogs [У собак]
https://coollib.com/b/146320/read#t61

The Silent [Молчащие]
https://coollib.com/b/146320/read#t104

Sunday Morning in the Forest [Воскресное утро в лесу]
https://coollib.com/b/146320/read#t157

Fantasy [Фантастика]
https://hendonpress.co.uk/lipkin-poems-from-the-original-russian/#fantasy

Thrush [Дрозд]
http://iknigi.net/avtor-semen-lipkin/30936-ochevidec-izbrannye-stihot-
voreniya-semen-lipkin/read/page-7.html

The Desert [В пустыне]
https://coollib.com/b/146320/read#t210

By the Sea [У Моря]
https://coollib.com/b/146320/read#t107

When I Was Putting Letters Into Words (I Was Accompanied By A Crazy Century) [Век сумасшедший мне сопутствовал (Когда в слова я буквы складывал)]
https://coollib.com/b/146320/read#t191

Two Mirrors [Два зеркала]
https://modernlib.net/books/semen_lipkin/ochevidec_izbrannie_stihotvoreniya/read_2/

Tao [Дао]
https://coollib.com/b/146320/read#t94

Time [Время]
http://www.peoples.ru/art/literature/poetry/contemporary/lipkin/poetry_vremja.shtml

The Monkey House [Обезьянник]
https://coollib.com/b/146320/read#t102

Conversation [Беседа]
http://coollib.com/b/146320/read#t17

Two Nights [Две ночи]
http://hram-aif.ru/stihi-na-vyhodnoj-10/